Sinister Wisdom 124
Spring 2022

Publisher: Sinister Wisdom, Inc.
Editor & Publisher: Julie R. Enszer
Guest Editors: B. Leaf Cronewrite, Barbara Esrig, Beth York, Gail Reeder, Lorraine Fontana, Merril Mushroom, Rose Norman

Graphic Designer: Nieves Guerra
Copy Editor: Amy Haejung
Board of Directors: Roberta Arnold, Tara Shea Burke, Cheryl Clarke, Julie R. Enszer, Sara Gregory, Shromona Mandal, Joan Nestle, Rose Norman, Mecca Jamilah Sullivan, Yasmin Tambiah, and Red Washburn

Front Cover Art: *Mystic Morning*
Artist: Robin Toler
Media: Oil Pastel on Construction Paper (2009)
Size of Artwork: 12" x 18"

Biography: Robin Toler is a board certified art therapist, licensed addictions counselor, and Advanced Integrative Therapy practitioner. Toler has a feminist private therapy practice which is located in Baton Rouge, Louisiana and is based on the principles of equity and human rights. Her expertise includes women's mental health, substance abuse, and trauma resolution. Toler continues to enjoy art making, drumming, writing, traveling, advocacy, and teaching. She can be reached at www.robintoler.com, andwww.robintolerartstudio.com

Robin Toler Artist Statement: *Mystic Morning* is a capturing, and a framing of feminist activism which has emerged outside of normal onsciousness, symbolizing the return of morning, associated with the resurrection of the sun and the hope of a new day. It points to a transcendental and other worldly and non rational understanding which relates directly to women's experience into their sacred rites, traditions, and rituals. This art piece represents the ineffable nature of lesbian experiences as being part nonliteral, part symbolic, and part arcane capable of conjuring up an ongoing spiritual mystery.

SINISTER WISDOM, founded 1976
Former editors and publishers:
Harriet Ellenberger (aka Desmoines) and Catherine Nicholson (1976–1981)
Michelle Cliff and Adrienne Rich (1981–1983)
Michaele Uccella (1983–1984)
Melanie Kaye/Kantrowitz (1983–1987)
Elana Dykewomon (1987–1994)
Caryatis Cardea (1991–1994)
Akiba Onada-Sikwoia (1995–1997)
Margo Mercedes Rivera-Weiss (1997–2000)
Fran Day (2004–2010)
Julie R. Enszer & Merry Gangemi (2010–2013)
Julie R. Enszer (2013–)

Copyright © 2022 *Sinister Wisdom*, Inc.
All rights revert to individual authors and artists upon publication.
Printed in the U. S. on recycled paper.

Subscribe online: www.SinisterWisdom.org
Join *Sinister Wisdom* on Facebook: www.Facebook.com/SinisterWisdom
Follow *Sinister Wisdom* on Instagram: www.Instagram.com/sinister_wisdom
Follow *Sinister Wisdom* on Twitter: www.twitter.com/Sinister_Wisdom
Sinister Wisdom is a US non-profit organization; donations to support the work and distribution of *Sinister Wisdom* are welcome and appreciated. Consider including *Sinister Wisdom* in your will.

Sinister Wisdom, 2333 McIntosh Road, Dover, FL 33527-5980 USA

TABLE OF CONTENTS

Notes for a Magazine 7
Notes for a Special Issue 9
The Goddess Chant 13
RITUAL THEATRE SCRIPT BY DIANA RIVERS
Sisters, Let Us Remember 15
BETH YORK
Transformations: Following the Muse 19
ROSE NORMAN
Pagoda-temple of Love 28
FLASH SILVERMOON
Creating the Rainbow Goddess Tradition 36
DEBRA L. GISH, FROM AN INTERVIEW WITH DIANA RIVERS
Diana Rivers: From Atheist to Pagan 41
CEDAR HEARTWOOD
Founding the Circle of Isis Coven 46
Candlemas 9984 48
Changes 50
JENNY YATES
She Changes Everything She Touches: Circle of Isis 51
GWEN DEMETER
Memphis Moonlodge 1980 55
MAYA WHITE SPARKS
A Witch's Memoir 56
KIM DUCKETT, FROM AN INTERVIEW WITH ROSE NORMAN
Shamanism and Feminist Spirituality 63
ROSE NORMAN
Ellen Spangler and Starcrest 67
KATHLEEN "CORKY" CULVER
A Croning on Women's Land 73
SAGE MORSE
From Convent to Coven . . . and Beyond 76

GAIL REEDER
    My Journey to The Dykes of Dungeness 81
JUDY L. MCVEY
    Christian Lesbians in the South 86
LORRAINE FONTANA
    Christians, Pagans, and Politics:
        Notes for a Spiritual Timeline from *Atalanta* 91
HELEN RENÉE BRAWNER
    Appalachian Quilt Magic 103
B. LEAF CRONEWRITE
    Wellsprings Festivals, 1995–97 109
ROBIN TOLER
    Becoming a Lesbian at Wellsprings Festival 112
BARBARA ESRIG
    Chocolate Cheesecake 114
MARILYN MESH AND BARBARA ESRIG
    Jewish Lesbian Support Group and Seders 117
MERRIL MUSHROOM
    Jewdyke in Shicksaville 121
LORRAINE FONTANA
    ALFA, AA, and the Spiritual Path 125
SUS AUSTILL
    Constant Craving: Sex, Safety, and Sobriety 127
HELEN RENÉE BRAWNER
    Getting Sober in AA 132
KATHLEEN "CORKY" CULVER, FROM AN INTERVIEW WITH BARBARA ESRIG
    I Get Dry with a Little Help from My Friends 135
WOODY BLUE FROM LORRAINE FONTANA'S INTERVIEW
        WITH CAROLYN MOBLEY
    Mobley-izing For Change:
        A Black Lesbian Seeking Community in the South 140
MERRIL MUSHROOM, FROM AN INTERVIEW
        WITH FELICIA FONTAINE AND BARB COLLINS
    Felicia and Barb and Bork:
        Lesbian-Feminist Activism in Alabama 147

PHYLLIS MEEK INTERVIEWED BY BARBARA ESRIG
   Phyllis Meek: Pioneer for Gender Non-Discrimination Policy .. 153
AN INTERVIEW WITH MARY ANNE ADAMS
   From Oxford, Mississippi, to Atlanta, Georgia:
   A Black Lesbian's Journey to Community 156
FROM AN INTERVIEW BY DANCINGWATER
   Eleanor Smith: Disability Activist 164
LAUREL FEREJOHN
   Inform, Inspire, Connect: Five Years with *The Newsletter* ... 168
DREA FIREWALKER
   Inspired to Honor Womonwriters Who Had Passed 171
LYRICS BY LENNY LASATER AND MENDY KNOTT
MUSIC BY LENNY LASATER
   These Friends of Mine 178
LENNY LASATER
   Writing "These Friends of Mine" 180

   The Southern Lesbian Feminist Activist Herstory Collection
   in *Sinister Wisdom* 182

   Snapshot Lesbian Love Celebration 189

   Book Reviews 193
   Remembrances 207
   Contributors 215

NOTES FOR A MAGAZINE

My feet were barely wet in the swimming pool of *Sinister Wisdom* when Rose Norman reached out to me about publishing some work from a group that called themselves the Southern Lesbian Feminist Activist Herstory Project. Rose wondered if *Sinister Wisdom* might dedicate an issue to the stories that they were researching and writing. My default response to inquiries that come to *Sinister Wisdom* is yes. Who does not want to say yes to projects that illuminate lesbian lives and lesbian culture? So I told Rose, yes. What I did not realize is that I was saying yes to an extraordinary partnership in the life of *Sinister Wisdom*—and for me personally.

The Southern Lesbian Feminist Activist Herstory Project is a gathering of women writers dedicated to preserving the herstories that the project names. A plucky, committed group of women, they now have produced collectively six issues of *Sinister Wisdom* and contributed enormously to our understanding of the lesbian-feminist south from the 1970s, 1980s, and 1990s. Over six volumes, these women have unearthed stories about organizing, activism, businesses, and other passionate community expressions and engagements of lesbian-feminists and lesbian-feminisms in the US South. Publishing this work in the pages of *Sinister Wisdom* has been a great joy.

As a part of the final installment of the series, *Sinister Wisdom* has produced a boxed set of these six issues. This boxed set is a limited edition; 50 boxed sets are available and they are already halfway to sold out. If you would like to order one, you can purchase one at www.sinisterwisdom.org/oralherstorians. *But there is more.* In addition to the lovely bookmark which every subscriber receives in the issue mailing, *Sinister Wisdom* has produced a poster that features the six covers of these issues. This poster is also for sale, in a limited edition, and available at www.sinisterwisdom.org/oralherstorians. Make plans to snag your copies of these items today before they run out!

The work of the Southern Lesbian Feminist Activist Herstory Project published in *Sinister Wisdom* is collaborative of many women, from named editors and authors within the issues to women interviewed and including many other named and unnamed contributors. This collaborative inspires me as I have seen many ways these women support and show up for one another, in creating the issues, promoting and celebrating the issues, and sharing their lives broadly to provide support, succor, and sustenance to one another. The majority of my work with the collaborative has been through Rose Norman; Rose has functioned as the general editor for the series and she has become a valued collaborator of mine. I appreciate her perspectives on a range of issues and value her opinions. She is also one of the kindest and most generous people I know. I hope that other activist formations have someone as dedicated as Rose to tell their stories in the future.

While it is bittersweet to reach the sixth and final installment of this series, it is also with an extraordinary sense of accomplishment and wonder. What work will the women of the Southern Lesbian Feminist Activist Herstory Project do next (besides their fabulous new website SLFAherstoryproject.org which launches with this issue)? What will future generations of women do with the stories gathered in these six issues? What other long-term project will come across my desk next that will blossom into such a wonderful collaboration? My mind and heart remain open.

In the meantime, I am looking forward to continuing to work with Rose Norman on her wonderful community biography of the Pagoda, a lesbian-feminist cultural space in Vilano Beach, Florida, and with other comrades from the project on a variety of other issues of *Sinister Wisdom*.

I hope you love this issue and more importantly that you imagine yourself in these pages. How would you like to contribute to *Sinister Wisdom*? How will you create, remember, and celebrate lesbian literature and art?

In sisterhood,
Julie
Julie R. Enszer, PhD
April 2022

NOTES FOR A SPECIAL ISSUE

*S*inister Wisdom 124: *Deeply Held Beliefs: Spiritual/Political Activism of Lesbian Feminists in the South* brings together the sixth and last issue of stories collected by the Southern Lesbian Feminist Activist Herstory Project (SLFAHP). Many of these stories show the intersection of spirituality and religion with politics and social justice movements in the South. This final issue is devoted to our spiritual paths, expressed through traditional religious practices and creative work led by spirit, and through political action guided by deeply held beliefs in social justice, the divine feminine, and commitment to preserving and defending Mother Earth.

While some political activists have regarded feminist spirituality as a diversion from a narrow view of politics, we see a strong intersection between the political and the spiritual. "Political" refers to the way we do our activism. In keeping with the definition of the word "politic," we try to be wise, prudent, circumspect, and discerning in our work as Southern lesbian-feminist activists. "Spiritual" refers to a way of thinking and behaving that goes beyond relating to our lives in terms of physical matters only, but instead relating in ways that are other than those of the material plane. Spirituality refers to the mind, the intellect, the soul. In a sense, our political work that relates to the physical world can be considered sacred, that is, of the soul, the vital force, essence, inspiration. Politics is practical; spirituality is intuitive. We as women are both practical and intuitive. Politics and intuition blend well in the work we do.

In general, the heteropatriarchy has been less than kind to us as women, as lesbians, as feminists, as activists and troublemakers. The fact that we are taking control of important aspects of our lives, our work, our selves makes the practice and the experience of spirituality a political act, while spiritual practices, rites and rituals, and a belief system can be comforting and can temper the intensity of our lesbian-feminist radicalism. Spiritual activism often involves rites and rituals that may be inherent, spontaneous, or deliberately constructed. Political activism involves direct causative action and can be overt or covert. In our Southern lesbian-feminist activism, the two are comprehensive; they both imply and contain each other. The intentions in our political acts are spiritual, while the practical manifestations of our spirituality are political. All of this is both contained in and constrained by the society in which we function.

In the 1960s, the South became the crucible for civil rights activism that developed and fed the lesbian-feminist activism of the last decades of the twentieth century. Throughout Southern states, lesbian-feminists were leaders in many kinds of social justice activism that often intersected with the religious and spiritual activism that was taking place in the women's movement all over the country. Lorraine Fontana traces this thread as it manifests in *Atalanta*, the monthly newsletter of the Atlanta Lesbian Feminist Alliance (ALFA). *Atalanta* reported on periodicals like *WomanSpirit*, a quarterly magazine published by Ruth and Jean Mountaingrove in Oregon from 1974–84, and the *Journal of Women and Religion* from the Graduate Theological Union in Berkeley, CA. ALFA wrote about the first openly lesbian bishop in the Episcopal Church (1977), the second Lesbian Gay Seminarians Conference, held at Harvard Divinity School in 1979, the "3rd World Lesbian and Gay Christian Conference" held in Washington, DC, and the first Catholic Lesbian Conference, held in Bangor, PA (both in 1982). They wrote about the backlash from organizations like The Christian Voice, an antigay lobbying group, and about protests against Jerry Falwell's Moral Majority. They reviewed books that were being reprinted about the subjugation of women by church and state, and about the new feminist spirituality, books like Merlin Stone's *When God Was a Woman*, Starhawk's *Dreaming the Dark*, and Barbara G. Walker's *The Women's Encyclopedia of Myths and Secrets*.

While we see spirituality and politics intersecting, we have divided them in this issue, beginning with stories we have been collecting for years under the heading "Rites and Rituals," most of them focusing on groups of lesbians. In this section, you will find lesbians founding goddess churches, a nun who became a witch, and several stories of covens, as well as Jewish lesbians who honored their religious traditions in a lesbian-feminist way, and a lesbian couple who found "Appalachian Quilt Magic" among country folk. We conclude this group with stories of individual lesbians in recovery through Alcoholics Anonymous, itself an organization that combines spirituality with politics, and here with a lesbian twist. A separate section on individual lesbian activists begins with two stories about MCC ministers, followed by the story of a university dean who pioneered gender nondiscrimination, a civil rights activist, a disability activist, and a newsletter editor whose story got left out of our last issue.

In the final essay, we tell the story of our ongoing Herstory Project, born in 2009 at Womonwrites: the Southeast Lesbian Writers Conference. All of the six special issues of *Sinister Wisdom* that we have published since 2014 owe a huge debt to Womonwrites. Founded in 1979, Womonwrites met annually for forty years, twice a year from 1997 to 2019. It drew lesbian writers from all over the Southeast, as far west as Louisiana and north to Kentucky, as well as from other parts of the United States and other countries. Those gatherings created the social networks that helped us find the previously untold stories that fill these special issues. We commemorate Womonwrites with Drea Firewalker's story of the Remembrance Project, installations that she created at Womonwrites honoring Southern lesbians who have passed before us, leaving a rich legacy of written and spoken word, and with a song by Womonwriters Lenny Lasater and Mendy Knott, "These Friends of Mine."

    B. Leaf Cronewrite
    Barbara Esrig
    Beth York
    Gail Reeder
    Lorraine Fontana
    Merril Mushroom
    Rose Norman

THE GODDESS CHANT

The Goddess Chant
by Phyllis Free ©1979

The Goddess rises within me

I am she who ever will be free

From trouble's hand she lifts me

I am she who ever will be free

The Goddess in me

Lifts me up and takes me to the sea

To cleanse and heal the wounds of

chains that bind me

The Goddess in me

I am she who is free

The Goddess in me

I am she

She is we

We are free

The Goddess Chant
Recorded by Beth York & Phyllis Free
CD SR © 2019 Beth York: Finding Home

Home Beach Blue image collage
Oil on canvas by Phyllis Free
with portrait photo by R. Gowen

Collage by Cat Purdom

ABOUT THE GODDESS CHANT

Phyllis Free wrote "The Goddess Chant" in 1979 and performed it with the lesbian band Anima Rising, in which she was drummer. Later she learned that the Atlanta women's spirituality group known as The Dykes of Dungeness (see their story pp. 78-82) had continued singing her chant for many years, without remembering its source. Working from Gail Reeder's unsigned, handwritten lyrics, they had credited it to "Anonymous" when they printed a songbook for the group. Even later, a chant collector now based in Canada included a recording of the chant in *her* collection, also without knowledge of the source. Now well within her crone years, Phyllis Free is proud to claim credit for her original composition, the manuscript of which is shown on the facing page, superimposed on a painting by Phyllis, beneath a photo of her. A recording of "The Goddess Chant" is now available as the opening track of Beth York's *Finding Home* CD, with djembe accompaniment by the author/composer.

Gail Reeder's handwritten but unsigned lyrics

SISTERS, LET US REMEMBER
Ritual theatre script by Diana Rivers

Sisters, let us tell the old stories again, so all is not lost and forgotten. Let us remember how it once was. I tell you it was not always as you see it now. Not always with grief and anguish everywhere and children crying.

Once there was another time, back, far back, back before war came into the world, before blade and gun and bomb bloodied our earth. There was a time when women walked in freedom, when children did not weep with fear and hunger.

Listen, my Sisters, my Brothers, those were golden years, years when the land lay fair and green under the sun and the Queen of Heaven reigned over all that was or ever had been. After the Great Goddess gave birth to the earth and its children, She Herself walked here among us in Her many guises and we followed in Her ways. Then life was bountiful and there was peace.

The daughters of earth walked with pride on sacred ground holding their heads high. Brother did not raise his hand against brother. The sons of the Mother did not grow up being trained to kill other mothers' sons. We used our gifts for living, not for death.

The pleasures of the body were a celebration of Her joy. In those days none spoke of sin and shame and evil. Children were a gift from Her for there was food enough and time enough and every child was a child of the Mother. We sang Her praises then and played our flutes and drums. We danced for Her in the village square by the noon sun. And in the sacred grove by moonlight.

Out of love we baked cakes for the Queen of Heaven and we poured out libations at Her shrines, for She was our life and our world. With what She taught us we learned to build cities of great beauty. We filled the temples with paintings and sculptures and mosaics in Her honor. There were no skills we did not learn save for the skills of war. Peace lived among us there for a thousand years and then a thousand more.

But what has happened to it now, that golden world, that time of peace and plenty? What has become of all the great cities where the Goddess was worshipped? The fabled cities of Crete were the last of Her cities, and even they are dust and ruins now. I ask you, where has it all gone?

Gone, all gone, gone under the sword, gone down in blood and fire. They came riding out of the north and out of the south, wave after wave of them with blood on their swords. They rode out of the waste places, the harsh dry places at the edge of the world bringing with them their gods of war and destruction, their angry gods of vengeance and of power. They were jealous of what we had made and came to plunder and destroy. They tore down our cities. Our streets ran with blood. With rage they toppled the stones of the temples, fouled Her shrines, and cut down the sacred groves. Nothing was as it had been. Joy was extinguished like a candle.

Under threat of death, we were warned to forget the old ways and bow to the new gods. The jealous angry gods were praised in Her place. Their temples were built over the ruins of ours. Years passed in wars. The story of that time is a long terrible story of conquest and pillage, of ruin and desolation and suffering beyond measure. It is the story they call history. We weep and we mourn for all those who went under the blade.

But some of us still remembered. In spite of their threats we kept to the old ways. We worshiped in secret places and still called on Her by Her many names. In our hearts we did not bow to the gods of blood and iron. We told our daughters and our daughters' daughters all that our mothers had told to us. We remembered when there was joy in the land and women had danced in the streets without fear.

We remembered as we endured through the long years of grief while men warred for greed and power and the children went hungry. We remembered as we tried to ease the suffering.

We remembered that there had been another time, that once the Goddess had ruled in peace and plenty, ruled for far longer than these men had ruled with steel.

We have not forgotten, no we have not forgotten. Listen, I hear a new wind blowing. It is time, it is time now. Things are changing again. The old knowledge is coming back into the world. Some of us are born with it. More and more of us are remembering. We are finding each other. We are making a web of knowing. The time of mourning is almost over. It is time for the killing to end, for the suffering to end, for the shame to be done with.

It is time to welcome the Goddess home now and make Her a place in the center of our lives. It is time to come back from our secret hidden places of worship and dare to say Her name aloud in the city street, dare to shout it to the heavens, dare to walk into the councils of men singing Her praises and dancing in Her honor. It is time to bring joy back into the public world. Never again will they make us ashamed of our minds, our bodies, and our souls. It is time for men to remember that they too are the children of the Mother. There has been enough of the bloodshed and the killing, enough of the cruelty and the lies. It is time to reclaim the earth for the living, time to remember how we once drank together from the cup of life, time to bring the Goddess home again. Time to bring the Goddess home again! Time to bring the Goddess home again! (Try to get the audience to join on the last few lines.)

Diana Rivers wrote Sisters, Let Us Remember *when asked to write what she learned from a class she took at the Unitarian Church. Goddess Productions performed it in many locations from the late 1980s to the early 1990s. Diana gives her full approval to perform this piece wherever the Goddess needs to be present. She only asks that performers give her credit and let her know when performing; this will greatly lift her spirits since she can no longer perform. Write Diana Rivers at 767 Madison 5524, Elkins, AR 72727 or* rivers5524@aol.com. *This piece and several others written and performed by Diana and her group are being gathered to publish via a Playbook. Prepared by Debra L. Gish, Author/Editor,* Crone Chronicles 20-20.

Black Goddess

TRANSFORMATIONS: FOLLOWING THE MUSE
Beth York

Atlanta, December 1980. Anima Rising has disbanded.[1] My spirit sinks. The band created dynamic, original music, but our voices clashed, fell silent. We couldn't speak to each other anymore. Differences emerged in music and life paths. I grieve and collapse into a void of lost connections, lost harmonies.

I grieve on many levels. My grandmother passes away, the woman who mothered me more than Momma ever could. John Lennon is killed on a New York sidewalk. I survive an abusive relationship and begin therapy. I retreat into an upstairs apartment.

>   Fly to a home in the trees
>   Buffeted by windstorm and thunder
>   Curl up, nested and scared,
>   Covered face with feathered wings.
>   Will this wounded songbird sing?
>   Will she wail into this night?
>   Will her attempts be lost to the winds?
>   Will she choke? Will she sing alone?
>   All of it.

I work as a clinical music therapist in a psychiatric hospital. I work with people who speak differently, learn differently, hear voices. The language I use is music. We are musical beings. The ability to perceive and interact with music is ancient and hardwired. We hear a rhythmic pulse and naturally move our bodies in time, catch a familiar melody, remember lyrics that accompany the melody, communicate, attach meaning. Music making is intuitive:

---

[1] *Sinister Wisdom* 104.

listening, moving, singing songs, improvising, drumming together evokes feeling. Music is my partner. We meet, trust each other. Music holds my clients. Music holds me.

A grand piano sits in the auditorium of the hospital. Between sessions my fingers travel randomly over the keys. I wander through possibilities pouring from my heart, trusting where fingers lead; find melody lines, major to minor modes held in time; become aware of repeated patterns, motives, dynamic motion. I move through these changes, explore new territory, improvise my way through complex emotions. For the next three months I gestate. Something new is taking form, turning me inside out. Judy hears me play piano at Womonwrites, May 1981. She listens, leans over, whispers, "Write it down."

Her words strike an insistent chord. I am dreaming sounds, hearing voices. Is what I hear *worthy* of being written down? Is it *good enough? Am I good enough?* I buy a pad and begin—tentatively, terrified of my own judgments—to notate the piano part. Note by note, from audiation to the piano to the page, resharpening the lead pencil; its eraser wears down to the metal casing. I commit, translating inner harmony and dissonance to notes on a staff. The music becomes my teacher, my healer, my provocateur. She guides me. I am opening, listening, transparent. Composing myself. I have never done this before.

New voices emerge. Strings, woodwinds, percussion. I hear them speak to each other. They pass, meet, blend, listen, move forward. The timbre of each instrument has a part to play. I slowly give birth to *Transformations*. Here is how I describe it in the liner notes to the Ladyslipper release:

> *Transformations* is a piece in five movements for chamber ensemble that explores the concept and the inevitability of change. The changes that occur within the music are emotional as well as instrumental and progress from anger and pain through humor and paradox & finally reach spiritual

reconciliation in the hymn-like finale. It is a piece that invites involvement and relationship . . . a musical expression dedicated to the spirit of transformation that lies within women everywhere—the spirit of personal liberty that urges us to take risks, explore our creative potential . . . the spirit that promotes the healing of wounds that have embittered us . . . transforming rage into reconciliation into vehicles for positive movement.[2]

How does the music sound? I find musicians who agree to help. We rehearse at the First Existentialist Congregation in Atlanta. I receive a call from Lucina's Music. They are producing flautist/composer Kay Gardner in September. We agree to open for her. I am ecstatic and terrified, honored. I consider Kay to be a role model. Kay contributed to *Lavender Jane Loves Women*, one of the first lesbian-produced recordings, then produced her own, *Mooncircles*. I met her at the 1st Congress of Women in Music in New York in 1980 and recalled her words from an interview with Gayle Kimball in 1981:

> I believe I have identified a "women's form" in music. I believe that women write innately and naturally in circular form and that the form parallels our own cycles . . . the problem with women composers is that we haven't had female role models. We, as women, are only beginning to identify our own forms.[3]

September 26, 1981. Lucina's Music concert with Kay Gardner and Beth York "performing with her chamber ensemble" at the Atlanta OIC Auditorium. My grandmother is there. Mother is

---

2 *Transformations*. Ladyslipper Music, 1985.

3 *Women's Culture: The Women's Renaissance of the Seventies* (Scarecrow Press, 1981), 164.

there. We are prepared, confident, and receive a standing ovation from 800 women. Kay is gracious, allows time after the concert for conversation. She has signed with Ladyslipper Records and asks, "Are you planning to record *Transformations*?"

Led by the muse, Lucina's sound engineer invites me to her studio to record each musician, part by part, movement by movement. She generously gifts me with her skills. Everyone does. I am forever grateful to everyone who shows faith in my work.

October 24, 1981. A second concert of *Transformations* at the First Existentialist Congregation. Subsequent concerts in 1981 and 1982 at the Atlanta Historical Society, the Atlanta Arts Festival. I play piano for Judy Chicago's Dinner Party exhibition at the Fox Theater, a benefit for Orchid Productions and the Atlanta Lesbian Feminist Alliance (ALFA).

June 1983. Jo Hamby and I travel to the National Women's Music Festival at Indiana University, Bloomington. By February, the recording of *Transformations* is completed. I have written several smaller works, one called "Time and Again" for oboe and piano. I meet an oboe player at the festival, and we play for the Classical Showcase. As we exit the stage, I hear someone ask, "When is the album coming out?" I leave a demo recording of *Transformations* at the Ladyslipper table. When we return to Atlanta, Laurie Fuchs, founder of Ladyslipper, calls, asks, "Where is Side 2? We would like to include your music in our catalogue." I am ecstatic. But there is no Side 2.

Back in Atlanta, women gather at Janet's studio to hear *Transformations*. We request donations to record Side 2 at a larger studio. Contributions pour in. I record an African American lullaby my grandmother sang to me, "Go to Sleep." We work on "Time and Again" and "Dolphinia," a piece I had written for Shannon Gordon and the Atlanta Dancers Collective, performed at the Atlanta Dance Festival. I am riding winds of opportunity and moved by the generosity of friends supporting me to make the recording a reality.

Abby Drew, an Atlanta artist, donates the cover art. By August 1, 1983, the master is completed. Cassettes are distributed through the Ladyslipper Catalog. The review reads: "restoring, exquisite, beautiful music." Orchid Productions produces *Transformations* on December 10, 1983, at the Cliff Valley Unitarian Church. We sell the album for the first time.

With support from Kay Gardner, Jo Hamby, Laurie Fuchs, and the Atlanta women's community, I return to the National Women's Music Festival, May 27, 1984. *Transformations* is performed on the Sunday Showcase with dancer Erika Thorne and instrumentalists whom Kay has located for me. Kay is premiering her opera *Women's Voices* with libretto by Gertrude Stein. Later I write:

> The music begins. My fingers tremble and fly over the keys. I am confident, secure. By the second movement I am transported. The sound is beautiful and cannot be contained. A smile spreads across my face that lasts until the finale. The audience rises. We bow and bow again. The applause continues. Kay Gardner emerges from the audience, walks down the aisle, a priestess in her long flowing robe, arms outstretched, embraces me. I move through the crowd to the green room where I sit, lower my head, and weep tears of joy. Taking it in.[4]

After the festival, I drive alone to Twin Oaks Farm in Virginia to join a women's retreat. I attend a writer's workshop led by Minnie Bruce Pratt. Her prompt: "Write a poem to someone with whom you have been in conflict." During the time of *Anima Rising* and *Transformations*, I survived lesbian domestic abuse. Music healed me from the chaos of a difficult time. I write: "You push my passivity, lack of courage. I fight to assert myself, you hard sounding, you push my buttons, I push you back, we hold each

---

[4] Journal, Beth York, May 27, 1984.

other down, powerless, rather than lifting each other up . . . all the while claiming love."

Poems from Twin Oaks Farm[5]

I walk alone unaided into thickening trees
Each step tested for obstacles
Brushing past branches and crackling twigs
Footfall constant in the moonlight.
My vision blurs,
I scour the periphery
Starry sky from left to right
From the Pleiades to the tips of my toes
Blinded by the night
Yet still move forward.
I turn the bend onto Twin Oaks Farm
As a star falls over the moon.

I hear a presentation at Twin Oaks by Women's Action for Peace and write:

> Bluefire women,
> Changing the course of the planet,
> We remember trials by fire,
> But the warmth of our messages,
> The sweet licks of our flames
> Will bend the iron dinosaurs.
> With the heat of our naming,
> They will change
> Or be consumed by the flame.
> Bluefire women
> Filling empty wells of longing

---

5 Ibid., May 29–30, 1984.

> Women of this planet
> Cry out in their dreams
> Hearing your song
> So long forgotten,
> So long remembered.
> Now in this time of trial by fire,
> We sing again the sweet licks of harmony
> Keeping these fires burning in our circles tonight.

In 1984, I sign with the Ladyslipper label. They will produce and manufacture the album of "Transformations." Jo Hamby becomes my manager and promotes my work. In May 1985, I perform the Southern Women's Music Festival, Campfest (Pennsylvania), and main stage at the 10th National Festival with dancers and musicians from around the country. Another standing ovation. This music, written to heal myself, is touching other women. I am being carried, uplifted.

In 1986, I perform *Transformations* at the International Women's Music Festival in Israel. Women composers and performers from all over the world have gathered. My piano performance of *Transformations* at Beer Sheva University is well received. Later, I share the stage with composer Pauline Oliveros in what is billed as a "magical night in the desert." Vera Goldman, a Jewish Indian dancer and spiritualist living in Tel Aviv, tells me that a "whole world is being created through our art." I want to believe her.

The next day a professor at the university drives me and another performer into the Negev desert to a Bedouin "village." Three women, dressed in black embroidered robes, share tea and stories of their lives during Israeli occupation. The Bedouin tribes have been forced into settlements similar to American Indian reservations. We sing. They share fresh baked pita bread from outdoor ovens. Later I write:

Is it the memory of exile, of families torn apart that makes you strong? Your souls torn from home, torn from the land, your desert land, land of your mothers and fathers who have wandered here to this covenant, this promise of home? Survivors through centuries, claiming land, parentage, faith, your right to journey, to find your place among coral skies and turquoise waters, terraced mountains, to the spirit that breathes her light, her radiant light upon this land.[6]

Courtesy of Beth York. Photo by Mike Brown. Cover art Abby Drue. Collage by Cat Purdom

Transformations album cover

Transformations expanded and transformed me. Composing gave me strength and took me to places I never imagined. I introduced the last concert of *Transformations* this way:

> Don't forget women who work long hours for little or no money, to bring women's culture to you. Jo Hamby, Orchid Productions, Lillian Yielding (Seven Stages Theater,

---

6 Journal, June 1986.

Women's Voices Series), the Southeastern Arts Media and Education Project, Laurie Fuchs, Ladyslipper Music, Linda Vaughn (Atlanta Feminist Women's Chorus), Janet Snyder and other talented sound engineers. Don't forget organizations like ALFA, Women of Wisdom, the First Existentialist Congregation, Charis Books, the backbone of our audiences. There would be no concerts without each musician here who brings life to the voices in my head. I thank each of you tonight. Without you, there are no recordings, no concerts, no audiences. If we are to survive as a women's culture, as a community, we must acknowledge and value each other's contributions. If we don't value each other, I am afraid no one else will.

PAGODA-TEMPLE OF LOVE

Rose Norman

Every day there is a song, every night a gift of love, every moon a celebration

With that quotation on their letterhead, a handful of women ran a lesbian intentional community and cultural center, the Pagoda, on Vilano Beach in St. Augustine, FL, from 1977 until the end of the twentieth century. If you didn't know about it, that's because it was one of those best kept secrets of Lesbiana, with ads in feminist newsletters, but otherwise running under the radar. Yet for over twenty years, Pagoda produced scores of women musicians in their fifty-seat theatre, plus original plays, art exhibits, workshops, and more—all by and about women.[1] An important reason for its longevity was that women of Pagoda had incorporated as a church, Pagoda-temple of Love. The temple/church would sustain their cultural work for those twenty-two years, and still exists as a 501(c)(3) nonprofit under a new name. You might say they lucked into it, or that the Goddess sent it to them. Their story illustrates the close relationship between feminist spirituality and lesbian-feminist activism.

Morgana MacVicar, one of the Pagoda founders, had been an activist since her college days and grew up in a political family.[2] Her father and great-grandfather had been in the state legislature, and her father's mother, Mamie Girardeau Eaton, was the first

---

[1] See also Merril Mushroom, "Pagoda Playhouse: The Glory Days," *Sinister Wisdom* 104 (Spring 2017): 126–29; and Merril Mushroom, "Pagoda-temple of Love: Lesbian Paradise (1977–Present)," *Sinister Wisdom* 98 (Fall 2015): 53–61.

[2] See also Morgana, "Morgana," Older Queer Voices: The Intimacy of Survival, ed. Sandra Gail Lambert and Sarah Einstein. https://olderqueervoices.com/2017/01/28/morgana-by-morgana/

woman elected to a statewide office in Florida (1928, the Railroad Commission). In 1966 her father was appointed a federal judge, the first to enforce integration in Florida. That same year, she started college at Florida State University (FSU), where she was active in student politics and became radicalized. In graduate school at FSU, in 1972, Morgana, Ynestra King, and others started the FSU Women's Center, where she and Dorothy Allison taught the university's first Goddess class.

After finishing a Master's in dance, Morgana met Rena Carney while working as resident counselor at a halfway house for women in Tallahassee. She had hired Rena as an ASL interpreter for deaf women at the halfway house. Rena, too, was in graduate school, studying speech and language pathology, and they became fast friends, partly because of their shared interest in the arts. They found that they had great rapport as performers, Rena with her training in theatre and Morgana with her training in dance. Together they would form Terpsichore, a dance theatre company based in St. Augustine, and then, in pursuit of theatre space for Terpsichore, they and their romantic partners, Suzanne Chance and Kathleen Clementson, founded the Pagoda.

Once they figured out that they wanted to create women-only space for their feminist cultural center on the beach (which had once been the Pagoda Motel), they had to figure out how to support it. Morgana's father told her that the only way for a women-only organization to get nonprofit, tax-exempt status was to be a church. Enter Toni Head.

Toni Head was a leader in Florida NOW who had studied feminist spirituality and female deities. After corresponding with Merlin Stone, author of *When God Was a Woman* (1976), Toni Head decided to establish a church based on feminist ideas. Here's what she said about it:

> Now the first reason for starting the church came from my memories as a child of just not being able to relate to this

male god. I thought how wonderful it would have been to see god as a woman and myself in her image. . . .

The second thing was . . . damn, those tax advantages are good. Why shouldn't the feminist movement have the same benefits as the Baptists and these other religious groups who are so often our enemies?[3]

Toni Head and other NOW women incorporated the "Mother Church" in March 1978. A year later, they offered their incorporated church to the Pagoda women, who took it over March 14, 1979. Toni Head was not at all interested in the Wiccan revival that was sweeping the country at that time, but she saw that what the Pagoda women offered would be a way for the church to continue.

Morgana and Rena were very definitely interested in Wicca and had been influenced by the writings of Z Budapest, widely regarded as the founder of the Feminist Spirituality Movement in the United States.[4] Z's Dianic form of Wicca emphasizes the Goddess (or Triple Goddess, maiden-mother-crone) and women-only gatherings or covens. Z started the Susan B. Anthony Coven in 1971, usually regarded as the first women-only coven in the United States. She was doing tarot readings at her small shop in

---

[3] Quoted in Vicki Mariner, " 'I Still Have a Lot of Anger' ...": An Interview with Toni Head," Tallahassee Feminist History Project, an undated newspaper clipping from Morgana's archives. Some of Toni Head's writings can be found in the Florida NOW archive at the University of Florida, Box 6, folder 2 (1976–83). Toni Head died in 1984, but I have not found further biographical information.

[4] Margot Adler traces the complex history of modern Pagan and Neo-Pagan beliefs (earth-based religions) in *Drawing Down the Moon* (Boston: Beacon Press, 1979; revised 1986 and 2001). Adler links feminist and other modern American Wiccan groups to Gerald Gardner's writings about witchcraft in the 1950s, brought to the United States in the 1960s by Rosemary and Raymond Buckland (see his *Witchcraft from the Inside*, 1971). Adler also identifies several other influences on the hundreds (possibly thousands) of covens that sprang up all across America in the 1970s and after. Feminist spirituality is one segment of that larger movement, by and large unorganized and existing under the radar in covens, moon circles, and other women's gatherings without any official existence.

Venice, California, in 1975, when she was the subject of a police sting. She was arrested, tried, and convicted of fortune-telling. While she did not seek to be arrested, she did strenuously seek legal redress and got her conviction reversed nine years later by the California Supreme Court, on grounds of freedom of religion.[5] A first step in that direction was that the same month that she was arrested, February 1975, she applied for official recognition of the "Sisterhood of Wicca" as a church. This became "the first incorporated feminist religion in 10,000 years."[6] In 1978, Toni Head's Mother Church became the second.

The Pagoda women changed the name to "Pagoda-temple of Love" and replaced the original credo with one incorporating principles of feminist spirituality. Their revised bylaws remained much the same, mainly changing "Board of Trustees" to "Circle of Wise Womyn," "Ministers" to "Priestesses," and setting the annual meeting for the first new moon after Hallowmas. Although it was a state-recognized church, the Mother Church did not have 501(c)(3) status when Pagoda took it over. They had to file federal paperwork, but by November 1979, Pagoda-temple of Love had tax-exempt status, the financial advantage that helped it to run a cultural center on a shoestring and keep their prices very low.

---

5   The Freedom of Religion Act. See Krista Schwimmer, "Z Budapest: Feminist Witch Who Fights Back," *Free Venice Beachhead*, August 1, 2014. https://freevenicebeachhead.com/z-budapest-feminist-witch-who-fights-back/.

6   See also Hilary George-Parkin, "When Is Fortune-Telling a Crime," *The Atlantic*, November 14, 2014, online only, https://www.theatlantic.com/business/archive/2014/11/when-is-fortunetelling-a-crime/382738/. Quoted from an unsigned story titled "Witch Trial," *Womanspirit* vol. 1 no. 4, 1975: 51. The Reformed Congregation of the Goddess, International (RCG-I) has claimed to be the first Goddess church to be both incorporated and to obtain federal 501(c)(3) (tax-exempt) status. Founded in 1983 by Jade River, RCG-I may just not know about the existence of the much smaller Pagoda-temple of Love, which has the paperwork for its incorporation in 1978 and its 501(c)(3) status in November 1979. According to Margot Adler, the RCG-I operated a Women's Theological Institute, trained and ordained priestesses, and had more than two thousand members when Adler was writing (*op. cit.*, p. 130). It published the quarterly journal *Of a Like Mind* for eighteen years, starting in 1983.

By then, thirteen women had put in $600 each to make a down payment on the building that became the cultural center and the legal location of Pagoda-temple of Love. Those thirteen signed paperwork to turn over that building to the temple, becoming members of the Circle of Wise Womyn. Now they no longer had to pay property taxes on the building or file income tax, they qualified for bulk-rate postage (essential for fundraising), and all the monthly contributions to Pagoda became charitable donations that women could take off their income tax. For the first ten years, anyone who bought a Pagoda cottage was expected to contribute $600 to the Center and to join the Circle of Wise Womyn.

Altar in the big room upstairs where rituals were held. Kathy Clementson made the satin vagina on a big canvas. Barely visible are masks used in ritual theatre. Except for cronings, these events were seldom photographed.

Having a church was not just a convenient business arrangement for these women. Indeed, the spirituality of the place is the main thing that many people remember about it. Morgana and others loved celebrating Hallowmas, the solstices, equinoxes, and other holy days of the Pagan year. Morgana particularly loved the myth of Demeter and Persephone, which had been one of Terpsichore's first theatrical productions. The Pagoda women often staged theatrical rituals to celebrate spring equinox and enjoyed retelling myths from a feminist perspective. Like many Wiccans, they were not committed to a particular system of beliefs, and usually devised their own ritual procedures. Morgana became their leader (and president of the temple board) through her commitment to making a success of the retreat and cultural center, but she never called herself a "high priestess" (or "high" anything, she asserts), and often others took the lead in rituals.

They were also not committed to particular garb or accoutrement, though they did love to wear robes for special occasions. For many Pagoda residents, the spiritual was inextricable from the daily life of the community. Some residents met weekly for group discussion and began every meeting by raising a cone of power and sending out a circle of protection to loved ones, temple supporters, and anyone else they felt needed it.

Spring equinox program with cover art by Morgana

It wasn't just the formal rituals usually held in the upstairs meeting room that made the Pagoda a spiritual place. Some musicians experienced the downstairs theatre in much the same way. Here is singer June Millington describing her memory of what it was like to perform at Pagoda:

Every time I went there, the show felt great. I felt like the women who were there were *really* hearing my music and receiving it in a spiritual way, and that was very important to me, because I was *really* growing in leaps and bounds spiritually, between Buddhism and everything I was learning about goddesses and matriarchy and all that kind of stuff. Really, really important for the expansion of my inner space. The fact that it was not so well known was really fabulous because I could just be there, and every time I went there I felt like a seed had been planted in the ground, and I could just hang out and not only watch it grow but be a big part of its growth.

Millington recalls that she and her girlfriend might stay there a week as payment for her performance:

They also had a *great* library, so I would read all of these books about women's lives. . . . It was fantastic! I would go into this sacred space, really, within a sacred space, within the larger women's music world. This was like a deep, deep, deep inner place, and that's how I experienced it. . . . It was like being in the center of a conch shell or something. And you could hear the echoes resounding from all of time, really, if you just listened. You could hear it, you could feel it, you could read it. I mean it literally, when I say I felt like I was a seed who was replanted every time I went there and got to grow and was nourished—that's not a metaphor.

Flash Silvermoon, another professional musician as well as a professional psychic and tarot reader, regarded herself as the "house band" for Pagoda, and often performed there for free, especially at special occasions like celebrations of Pagoda's birthday. A video from their eighteenth birthday celebration (July 1995) shows Flash singing "Dancing with a Snake," a song she wrote for Morgana, with Morgana belly dancing to it (the snake is imaginary).

Four years later, Pagoda-temple of Love sold the building to a group of lesbians who had formed another nonprofit corporation, but it was not a church. Much as they tried and wanted the cultural center and retreat to continue, they could not make a go of it. When Pagoda-temple of Love left, taking the church with them, something very central to what kept the place going left, too. They had many reasons for leaving, not least of which was the wish for more space to expand. They had big dreams.

Morgana continued as president of what became Temple of the Great Mother, combining the two previous names. She and others had great plans for the seventy-six acres of beautiful Alabama mountain property that the temple bought adjacent to their new lesbian intentional community, Alapine, which is privately owned. At first, they saw it as the fulfillment of a dream they had had since the early 1980s: Crone's Nest, a retirement home for aging lesbians. In the early days, they held ritual circles on the temple land, which has no roads or utilities and so is not accessible. They still hold occasional circles, as well as memorials when they lose a beloved community member. For various reasons, their Crone's Nest dream did not manifest. Nowadays, its main project is placing monthly orders for the Alapine community to Frontier Co-op Wholesale, much as the natural food store used to do at Pagoda. In that respect, the temple still nourishes lesbian-feminist community.

Lavender and Morgana participating in a croning in 1983. Cronings and celebrations of the eight major holidays were held upstairs, where they maintained an altar as well as guest rooms. Lavender was a lawyer and Pagoda resident who did much legal work for the temple, including that for 501(c)(3) status.

CREATING THE RAINBOW GODDESS TRADITION

Flash Silvermoon[1]

My spiritual path is one I have walked for forty-five years. Under the name of Witch, Shaman, Healer, Pagan, and Goddess worshiper, I have understood more each day from the teachings of Wicca, Yoruba, Native American, feng shui, and Tantric. These teachings have led to the creation of the Rainbow Goddess Path. We honor diversity through many traditions, embracing each unique part and holding sacred that which resonates. We celebrate the Goddess in all her guises.

I live and work at Moonhaven in Melrose, FL, where I hold classes in tarot, astrology, stone healing, animal communication, and women's spirituality. With my music and shamanic ways, I practice my craft and share it with others. We walk the path together.

The first big women's event I hosted in the Gainesville area was Womanspirit Rising. It began one night in April of 1990 when I was nudged awake by the deep voice of the Spirit demanding me to gather women together. "Okay," I responded, "in the morning." "Now," she commanded. There's no arguing with that "get up and do it right now" kind of thing, so I started work immediately.

By midmorning I had studied the stars and found the perfect date to connect many other women with the transformative energies of the Moon and the Outer planets. I called Jordan Goodman at Kanapaha Botanical Gardens in Gainesville, and she was thrilled at the thought of using the garden to raise energy. With her daughter, she gave wholehearted support, and the date was set: July 10, 1990.

---

[1] Flash died of complications from diabetes December 15, 2017. The original draft of this story was based on Barbara Esrig's interview with Flash on March 6, 2017, revised for publication by Woody Blue, then rewritten by Flash in August 2017.

My next task was the most important. I had to find the right priestesses and leaders for such an undertaking. I needed a group of Rainbow Goddess–centered women to anchor the circle and raise the power. I chose Bahira Sugarman, who identified as a Jewitch Buddhist, to stand at the eastern corner to command the powers of Air. I decided to position myself in the south to bring the Fire element and also to control the flow of the circle. In the west, Georg Suzuki agreed to bring the Water element, calling on her Native American work.

The priestess of the north was the most difficult. I felt I needed an African priestess to call the Earth element and balance the circle. Unfortunately, I didn't know any, but the Goddess would provide. Through Arupa, a Gainesville friend, I connected with Babalosa, a local Yoruba priest, and he, in turn, connected me with Ayoka, a practitioner of the Yoruba faith, centered in the traditions of her Nigerian ancestors. After consulting her grandmother Omi Aladora Ajamu, who understood the importance of this gathering for all woman, Ayoka agreed, and the circle was complete. This was the beginning of my long and rich connection with the Yoruba African community.

When the day of the gathering arrived, I had done no advertising, yet 350 women of every path, age, and color showed up. We also drew interest from the *Gainesville Sun*, who showed up to document the event with photographers. We decided to send them away. We wanted to protect our women's private space, not a news story.

Ayoka and I began drumming and chanting on the hill as hundreds of women and girls streamed in, finding their place in the circle. Priestesses on each side welcomed them, smudging them as they entered the sacred space. Jordan and her daughter Summer offered sprigs of herbs, and the air was fragrant and filled with anticipation. I remember it like it was yesterday. The owl hooted in the east just as Bahira called in the energies of Air. The circle became suspended in time, and we all felt our cosmic connection.

The element of Fire was easy to call. It was 90+ degrees and the sweat was pouring off my face as I implored Fire to join us and led the group in the chant: "We All Come From the Goddess." Georg then welcomed the energies of Water with a Native American chant. Ayoka called to Earth and then offered prayers to the Ancestors as the hawks circled above us like a blessing.

I had written a segment for women to share in the middle of the ritual called "The Ancestors Speak." I chose women whose cultural heritage represented many different places. For instance, Corky, a poet, spoke a short verse from Sappho, and Denise Mathews, a Greek woman, dressed in a tunic and spoke the words of Artemis.

The whole event took almost three hours and was incredibly uplifting. As the women left in single file from the sacred space, Ayoka and I drummed and sang the Yoruba chant "Tumbo Lo' Run," thanking the spirits and inviting them to leave.

My mind was blown. This amazing event that had come to me in the middle of the night had been brought to completion. Everything had fallen into place so effortlessly, which was confirmation indeed.

Everyone was excited to do another gathering, and soon. Womanspirit Rising was the first of five big circles. For each circle I endeavored to do some Goddess teaching in connection with the Holy day we were celebrating. For Winter Solstice, a group of women shared the myth of Amaterasu, the Japanese Sun Goddess, whose rising sun symbol is still seen on Japan's flag. I used the same format for each circle, spreading power around to many women and traditions to bring peace and harmony.

The last Womanspirit Rising featured a day of workshops and a circle at night. It was quite ambitious, and the enormity of that job knocked me out enough to say, "I think I'll do my own projects for a little while."

And so I turned my attention to completing the Wise Woman's Tarot deck, which brought Goddesses from all over the world together. Barbara Vogel illustrated my visions, and the deck was published on Halloween 2002, the culmination of a twenty-five-year project. Tara Silverfox published and edited this project and the accompanying book.[2]

For many years I attended and performed at women's music festivals. But these events lacked the spiritual center I felt was important. That gave rise to the Wisewoman's Spirituality and Music Festival. Not only did I produce it, but I also performed and led workshops for all eight years. Seven of those were held at the Peace Camp near Waldo, FL. One year it was held at my home.

These were wonderful days of women coming together. It was amazing for women to feel that safety and space, and the knowledge shared was incredible. Billie Potts came and taught some great herbal classes. A sweat lodge was orchestrated by the Native American women, including Aurora Whitebird, Butterfly Circle Woman, and Songdancer. That was very popular. Lots of different women shared and brought amazing offerings.

Each gathering was unique. My band, The Blues Sisters, always played and was joined by Omi Aladora Ajamu, Denise Burnsed, and many of the musical Priestesses, so spirit and art and music merged and blessed and healed us all.

Flash Silvermoon at Moonhaven

Photo courtesy of Flash Silvermoon

---

2 This tarot deck is still available through various feminist retailers, including Aurora Collins's Crow's Crossroads Shoppe and Metaphysical Center on Facebook and at https://crowscrossroadsshoppe.com, and Sharon Julien's online shop Midnight Oracle, https://www.etsy.com/shop/MidnightOracleShop.

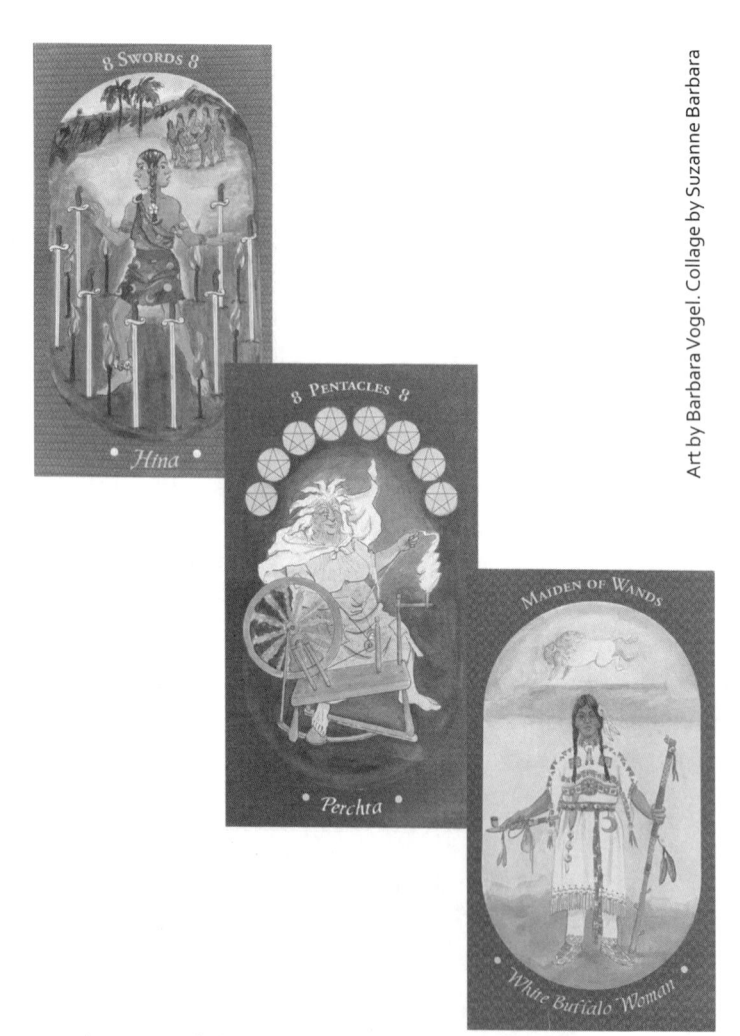

Art by Barbara Vogel. Collage by Suzanne Barbara

In keeping with the Rainbow Goddess tradition, the images on the Wise Woman tarot cards draw on many cultures. Sugarloaf artist Barbara Vogel, known as Vogel, painted the images guided by Flash. Flash writes about that process and includes color images in her 2009 obituary of Vogel, http://www.ata-tarot.com/reflections/04-05-09/barbara_vogels_journey_home.html.

DIANA RIVERS: FROM ATHEIST TO PAGAN
Debra L. Gish, from an interview with Diana Rivers[1]

Diana Rivers dove into the deep end, swimming into her new life upstream and against the current, but she was excited. She was free to explore and expand in ways she'd never dreamt of. We sat together on Diana's eighty-eighth birthday in front of the fifty-foot-long stone wall she built herself that is the back wall of her house. On this crisp October day, I marvel at her beauty. After surviving a near-fatal stroke five short years ago, she does not miss a beat. Vivacious as ever, Diana is a mystery, serious, purposeful, even a bit intimidating.

Leaving a twenty-year marriage after bearing three sons, Diana arrived in Arkansas divorced and alone in 1972, but with the resources to buy land. At thirty-eight, Diana was an atheist with no affiliation to anything spiritual. She wasted no time. With a young boyfriend, that same year she started Sassafras, originally a mixed land, counterculture community of both men and women, mostly hippies, where she flirted briefly with Buddhism but found nothing there to affirm her female self.[2]

In a few years, most of the women at Sassafras left and came out or came out and left. Following an explosive meeting, Sassafras became women's land. While there, Diana met a younger lover who was involved in spiritual circles. Diana didn't seek anything religious, but she was drawn to drumming circles, where she could stand outside in the forest with other women and the natural world. Though not the high Priestess, she helped to keep these

---

[1] Debra L. Gish interviewed Diana Rivers in her home at the Ozark Land Holding Association (OLHA) about thirty miles southeast of Fayetteville, AR, on her eighty-eighth birthday, October 17, 2019.

[2] See Merril Mushroom, "Arkansas Land and the Legacy of Sassafras," *Sinister Wisdom* 98 (2015): 36–45.

sacred circles going for a long time. A lifelong artist and sculptor, Diana also began to create full-bodied Goddess statues!

Born Diana Smith, then Diana Folley by marriage, she wanted a new name of her own choosing that would reflect moving into her new life and a new state. She loved the name Diana, chosen by her parents, saying she would have chosen it even if they had not, because Diana is the Goddess of the Forest and Wild Creatures. She wanted to change her surname to something more earthy, but not so new age that it would embarrass her later. She considered Forest and Rivers and decided that Rivers naturally flowed with Diana. Now she loves seeing it on her books.

"I didn't really have a Christian upbringing, but for some reason, when I was twelve, my mother decided I should be baptized. I don't know why. She never went to church herself, but I was pushed into a Wednesday afternoon Bible class." Diana rolls her eyes as she remembers going to two sessions before being thrown out. She recalls it was caterpillar season, and she was bored. She put caterpillars down the necks of girls sitting in front of her with hysterical results. The second time, she brought in a baby robin and worms. She was asked to leave the class before she did any major harm. "Don't remember if I ever did get baptized, but if I did, it sure didn't take!"

After attending a course at the local Unitarian Church called "Cakes for the Queen of Heaven," Diana immediately began looking for Goddesses in the Bible. For the last class, Diana wrote "Sisters, Let Us Remember," a piece of writing that was passed around with each woman reading one line. This became the first performance piece for Goddess Productions, a traveling reader's theatre that Diana started in the late 1980s and ran for five years into the early 1990s.

Afterward, she wrote several more scripts for reader's theatre and found ways to perform them. At first, she just did it on her own, but after a while, a collective of four was formed. They would go to women's communities in different places in Arkansas,

Florida, and Alabama, enlisting readers, drummers, dancers, and, if they were lucky, a flute player. After a couple of rehearsals, they would put on a show. They could do it so quickly because they were working from scripts; no memorizing was necessary. Some of the titles were "Nothing Tame," "Dancing the Spiral," "She Is Born," "Voices," and "Sisters, Let Us Remember" (see this issue).

In 1987, while sick in bed, she began writing a fantasy novel about a tribe of lesbian warriors with superpowers and mindreading abilities who are being hunted and need to learn to live together without conflict. She called them the Hadra. Often guided by an inner voice that wakened her at night, she continued to write their story in what became a seven-novel series, *The Hadra*.

During that time, the state university in the town near her home decided to have a long weekend Women's Conference and Festival. They asked for proposals. Diana recalls, "My friend Georgia and I wrote a wonderful one for a women's art show that we called WomanVision, but I think it sounded too radical for the students. We probably used the word *goddess* or talked about home altars, and the students turned us down." (However, Diana did end up curating the women's art show and continued that for the ten years of the conference.) "Angry and hurt, I was in Kansas City visiting my friend Laura and storming about this refusal. Laura said, 'Why don't you do WomanVision here in Kansas City?' I said, 'I don't live here, and besides, where would we do it?' " So, Laura took Diana to a place that accepted her idea.

They formed a collective of friends, and for the next three years, from 1991–1993, Diana spent part of the winter in Kansas City doing WomanVision very successfully each March. It was a dream come true. Diana says, "The WomanVision art show became the womb for every sort of woman's expression—spoken word, music, dance and whatever else we could think of, including Goddess Productions performances, of course."

WomanVision was followed in a couple of years by Matriarts, another art and performance women's venue, started by a friend.

This ran for about three years. After that, Diana had a longing to see women-centered art on the walls and kept talking about Goddesses, Angels, and Amazons. One evening after everyone came in from a full moon float on their local river, Diana asked her friend Vick if she would like to join her in producing a Goddess Festival. Vick said, "Sure!" Neither one knew what they were signing up for, but the Goddess Festival did happen. It started in 2009 with Diana at the helm for about five years, and it is still going. It used to be a month long, but now runs part of a week with a Spring Equinox ritual in the middle.

Diana Rivers

Courtesy of Go Strealy

Diana is sorry that she never got to build a Goddess Temple in the town near the women's land community where she has lived the last forty years, OLHA (Ozark Land Holding Association). But she boasts of a beautiful Goddess ritual space in a cedar grove on that land in the hills of northwest Arkansas. Diana has been exploring the questions of ritual and of MotherLove as the driving engine for evolution for a long time, including in her novels, stories, Goddess performance pieces, personal reading of history and anthropology, and many discussions with her friends and colleagues. She is committed to keeping the Goddess spirit alive, yet she no longer wants to lead. Now she is content to just participate and follow the rituals, all still so central to her blessed life as an authentic pagan Goddess.

FOUNDING THE CIRCLE OF ISIS COVEN

Cedar Heartwood

Isis, an Egyptian Goddess, was the one we chose to represent our coven when we formed. I fervently wish the news media would stop taking Her name in vain by calling the terrorists in Syria an acronym that sounds and spells the same. Outside the United States, they use ISIL in the English language press.

In the early 1980s, a woman visited the DC/Arlington area and held a workshop in someone's home. She was teaching about the Goddess, leading meditation, encouraging us to reconnect with our roots—our ancient roots, from before the patriarchy's complete takeover. I ended up with the sign-up sheet circulated during the meeting. Thinking out loud, I said, "I guess this means we are starting a circle here."

I called everyone on the list, and we set a meeting for the next month. It was like a "learntogether" because none of us knew much about rituals, guided meditation, or the names of the Goddess and what they all stood for. On the full moon prior to the quarter and cross-quarter days, we would meet to plan out our celebration, who would be crone this time, mother, and nymph, who would be gatekeepers, who would call the directions; what would be the theme or work of this circle, based on the season and what we were feeling. We very loosely followed Z Budapest's *The Book of Lights and Shadows*. We always had a scribe who added these proceedings to our own book.

On Candlemas 1983 we initiated each other into the Circle of Isis. We had ordered matching rings with our symbol on a flat silver oval. A lesbian jeweler made our rings with our symbol, a naked woman with wings spread, chalice on her belly, and arms holding the moon above her head.

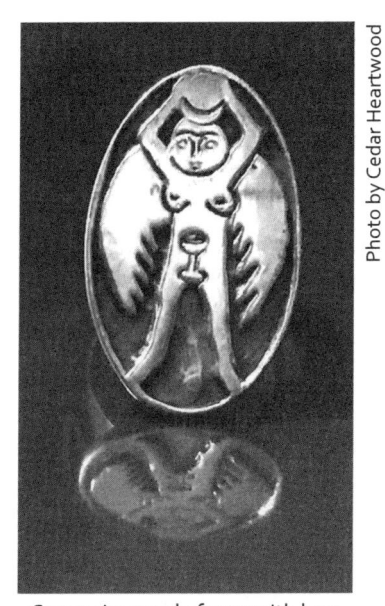

Coven ring made for us with love by Judy Winsett.

Photo by Cedar Heartwood

There were thirteen of us, and the ceremony started with calling the corners to set up a sacred circle. Four witches had researched a goddess to call for the East, South, West, and North, and composed an invocation to bring her into the circle. The gatekeepers normally face each other beside the altar to the East, arms raised to form an arch, welcoming each woman with a challenge and a kiss. This time, they stood naked in the dark with legs wide, starting a line through which each of us would be pulled. The challenge was presented with an athame (ceremonial knife) to the chest: "How do you enter the circle?" Ideally, the new member answered, "In perfect love and perfect trust." Some needed to use the adjective "growing" instead of "perfect." As each woman slid through the symbolic birth canal, she stood to add herself to the line and pull the next sister through. We entered oldest first.

With all of us inside the sacred circle, chanting and singing began. The crone for this ceremony placed each one's ring on her finger. As the voices died down, we entered deep meditation with Isis. At the end, dancing and drumming until it was time to thank the Goddesses from each direction and open the circle.

"The circle is open but unbroken. Merry meet and merry part, and merry meet again."

CANDLEMAS 9984

Cedar Heartwood

Today I face my first birthday as a witch
A year ago, I said
"Yes, I have the courage to walk
with the Goddess!"
Persephone said,
"Be soft and open
Vulnerable to the inner child
Find that child within and
Claim her."
Hecate said,
"If you don't need it, throw it out!
This one causes you pain
(see how it hurts)—throw it out!
Be strong and tough
and stand by yourself
Find the fierce Mother inside and
Claim her!"
What happened?
I cracked open
I broke in a million pieces
Vulnerable to all who knew me
The child had no more armor
I screamed and cried
and drove away what I loved
yet did not need
I was driven, too—
backed into the last corner of my own truth
Reluctantly, I stood my ground.
And now?

I'm alive
my body is whole
my mind gathers a form about her
my heart cries often
my spirit soars, I think,
but I cannot feel her.
It's been a year,
And I want to know, Goddess,
have I set sail in my own tiny boat
to explore your seas in hurricane season?
Goddess, where is the rudder,
Do you have any oars?

CHANGES

Cedar Heartwood

Oh the joy, the joy
of jumping off cliffs!
A rush of air
To wash away fear
breathing free . . . breathing free.
New earth I land on
uncharted in my mind
New water I splash through
waves of feeling break through me.
Tunnel of time, passage by fire
Consciously I quake
at the sight of lifetimes behind
Unconsciously, my soul smiles
the puzzle to reveal.
Old pain, old patterns
That hold me to the wheel
New lives and friends drawn
'round in circles
by that frozen rim
My soul asks me
to let go
to swing free of the wheel
jump off the cliff . . . in joy.

SHE CHANGES EVERYTHING SHE TOUCHES: CIRCLE OF ISIS

Jenny Yates

There are times when you leave an old life behind and move toward something very different. Thirty-three years ago, Circle of Isis made that possible for me.[1] It was not just a circle, but a threshold, and when I crossed it, I shed my skin. And then I grew another life, a life that centered on women.

It was the early '80s. I was thirty-one, a postal clerk living in the burbs of DC, with an eleven-year-old son. I was a feminist with lots of good woman friends, but my past relationships had been with men. I had crushes on women, but they didn't seem to respond to me in that way.

Back then, at the women's bookstore Lammas, you could pick up a little woman's newspaper called *The Crescent*. It was here I saw the announcement for a healing circle. I'd read a lot about women's spirituality—*The First Sex*, by Elizabeth Gould Davis; *When God Was a Woman*, by Merlin Stone—and thought I'd check it out.

And so I went to Jes and Kate's house in Arlington for the first time. At the healing circle, there were perhaps ten women, and we split into two groups. Every woman took a turn lying on a mat on the floor, her eyes closed, soaking up energy and attention from the women around her. She would say what she needed—maybe quiet touch, maybe jokes, maybe to tell her story. We laid gentle hands on her body, listened to her, sang songs, and told her that she was beautiful, strong, and brave. For every woman, it was different.

In that first healing circle—and there were many more later—I first heard Jes sing a song called "My Sisters," and I felt tears

---

[1] This is the same Circle of Isis as in the preceding story.

coming to my eyes. I felt that I had heard that song in some other lifetime, surrounded by women. It seemed that I had lost these women, and now I was returned to them.

Talking to the women afterwards, I found out about the coven, Circle of Isis, and I was invited to the next ritual, for the spring equinox. I was asked to bring two symbolic objects, one that encouraged the creative process and one that blocked it, and so I brought a candle and a candle-snuffer. In a circle of perhaps a dozen women, we shared our objects and the stories behind them. Afterwards, we threw off our clothes and danced, with women drumming and shaking rattles around us.

I went to many Circle of Isis rituals after that and became close to the other members. In that circle, I found both friends and lovers, and started calling myself a lesbian for the first time. And a year or so after that first ritual, I was initiated into the coven.

The coven had rituals eight times a year, at the quarters and cross-quarters. Sometimes it was just the members, while other times the whole community of women was invited. The coven itself was small, only five or six women, fluctuating as women joined us or moved away. The community of lesbians and spiritual women was large, but still, each ritual had a certain intimacy.

The coven was held together by the creativity of its members. Two weeks before a ritual, we'd meet at a planning session called an Esbat, and throw ideas around. We shared what we were working on, personally and spiritually, picked a theme—such as balance, joy, justice, peace, or transformation—and figured out ways to dramatize it, to make it real and to feel it in our bodies.

Sometimes we drew, wrote, or constructed things, and sometimes there were masks or other costumes. Sometimes we concentrated on a particular goddess, or a mythical being, and worked out ways to invoke her. Often there were props, like fire, water, staffs, or (once) balloons. Once, in a ritual about balance for the fall equinox, we constructed a balance beam and we all walked across it.

There was no set hierarchy in these rituals. Women volunteered for the position of Crone, Mother or Maiden, depending on how they felt at the moment. The Crone made sure that the ritual moved along, while the Mother took care of materials and practical concerns. The Maiden made sure that everybody had fun, and she could be silly if she wanted. Sometimes the Coven did very deep work, and the Maiden would be solemn, but she was the one who lightened the energy again afterwards.

Although Jes' and Kate's house was a frequent location, we met at different people's houses in Northern Virginia. Once there was a Spring Equinox ritual at my house with the theme of Blossoming, and we represented this with abundant flowers. My home was filled with them. This was an open ritual, and it turned out that a new woman—who hadn't been at the planning meeting—was highly allergic to flowers. There was no hesitation. We all immediately took all the flowers and carried them outside, and then went on with the ritual with imaginary flowers.

One thing I loved about the Circle of Isis was that feelings always came before protocol. If we needed to stop everything and let a woman cry, then we would do that. Everyone would gather around and embrace her. And this happened more than once, since the rituals were often very personal.

The spontaneity and creativity made every ritual different, even though there were certain steps that were common to all of them. We always had tables at the four directions with ritual objects, and there was an eclectic mix of different things from different women. The altars, lit with candles in a darkened room, were beautiful.

We always entered the circle through a gateway, formed by the arms of two women, and were then hugged by all the women who were already in the circle. By the time the ritual began, we were already in an altered state from all the hugs. We always "called the corners," invoking energies from the east, south, west and north, and usually one woman would prepare something to say at each direction. But other women would chime in, and we all said whatever we needed to say to the goddesses of air, fire, water and earth.

Along with meditating, singing, and raising energy, the rituals always had some time for sharing, either during or after the ritual work. We listened to each other, focusing our energy on each woman in turn, creating a field of trust and acceptance. In that sacred space, protected by ancient goddesses, there was room for self-knowledge, for new feelings, and for transformation.

The coven survived for many years, changing as people left and other people joined. For me, it was perhaps hardest when Jes and Kate left town for the womyn's land they had championed and saved for. The year after they left, I moved to Venezuela with my lover, and started working full-time as an astrologer. Without the Circle of Isis, I don't think I would have had the courage to break so completely with my old life. But when I came back to the United States in the summers, I found the coven was a little different every time, with fewer lesbians. Eventually, there were no women that I knew well, and I didn't stay in touch. This is something I regret now.

Just eight years ago, my lover (now my wife) and I returned to live in the States. I thought I would find another coven like Circle of Isis, but that hasn't happened. And now it is clear to me how beautiful and generous it was, and how it just appeared for me, exactly when I needed it, giving me power, magic, space, and support.

MEMPHIS MOONLODGE 1980

Gwen Demeter

We began with four wimmin and two kids on full moon and new moon: me, my partner Gail Atkins, Alycia B., and Carol S., plus her two boys. Brooke Medicine Eagle came to town for the Harmonic Convergence at Nexus Spiritual Land, where we hooked up with Emily F. and Jackie W., and others. I remember a full moon ritual at Lone Star Farm in a field with the cows peacefully grazing all around us!

Ceremonies began with calling the directions and singing songs to the goddesses, then raising energy for the ceremony's purpose. New women were brought in, and friends and family who needed healing, both male and female. Healing was generally through laying on of hands. The new moon rituals were for new projects, and for changing directions in a woman's life. Full moon rituals often centered on healing ourselves and generating energy to help heal the world's suffering.

There was a lesbian–straight split at one point. Some of the straight women thought there were too many new lesbians! This was at the same time that a spiritual teacher, a man, was in the apartment hot tub waiting to "teach" us. Some straight women started their own group; some stayed with us. We grew to about fifteen to twenty women, some of whom stayed connected and involved for the last thirty-five years. Lately we meet less, on a Saturday near the full or new moon.

From our group we have had five children born, several grandchildren, several new jobs, a wimmin's bookstore (Meristem in Memphis), and two Unitarian ministers. We have held six croning ceremonies and lost three members to death. We held a ritual for one woman the night before she died, as her ex-lover arrived to be by her side.

A WITCH'S MEMOIR

Maya White Sparks

Dedicated with gratitude to the witches of the Lesbian Feminist Dianic Coven, PTWs[1]

The room was glowing, with yellow-gold candle flames illuminating naked women's bodies. In a dreamlike state, I felt as if I were floating above the hands of my coven sisters. They had pulled me through a Goddess birth canal created by their open legs and then surrounded me, levitating me with a chant and their fingers beneath me as I lay prone. It was the late 1970s, and I had completed the traditional "year and a day" of training. With this ceremony, I was now an initiated member of a lesbian-feminist Dianic coven in Washington, DC: PTWs.

Connecting with this coven felt so perfectly right. As I look back on my good fortune, I am amazed and so grateful to the Fates for arranging it. Several years earlier, as a fledgling dyke in a Matriarchal Study Group at the Women's Center at the State University of New York (SUNY) at Oswego, I had set myself upon a path of studying the old Goddess religions. Later, inspired by the writing of Robin Morgan of W.I.T.C.H., The Women's International Terrorist Conspiracy from Hell (founded in 1968), I had self-initiated by saying three times, "I am a Witch!" With the help of a lecture by feminist theologian Mary Daly (who spoke at SUNY Oswego while I was there), I had been examining the impact of my twelve years of Catholic schooling and of living in a patriarchal

---

[1] During my time with PTWs, I was known as Toni White. Here is a partial list in alphabetical order of my spiritual mothers, the members of PTWs while I was celebrating with them: Alda Curtis, Aradia, Flo Hollis, Joan E. Biren (JEB), Lenora Trussell, Morgan Gwenwald, Toni Rees. Unfortunately, it is still not safe for some of us to be identified as witches, and so not everyone is listed here.

society. I had come to know that women's spirituality, sexuality, language, and the politics of power were intertwined, and there I was, diving into a Key Cauldron of Transformation of the Times, being stirred by the Great Goddess, activated for a Revolution in Human Consciousness.

PTWs gathered at Full Moon Esbats to plan our celebrations (rituals) for the major Sabbats, the solstices, equinoxes, and cross-quarter festivals (Beltane, Lammas, Hallowmas, and Candlemas). It was revolutionary not only to utilize the transformational energies of Nature's Wheel of the Year and to reclaim our psychic abilities; it was revolutionary the way in which we did it. The PTWs developed a group process that reflected feminist ideals of equality and shared power. Unlike most other pagan groups, there was no High Priestess or Priest running the show. Instead, we planned the rituals as a group, and for each ritual we rotated the major tasks, identified by the Triple Goddess titles of "Nymph" (she made sure everyone was having a good time), "Maiden" (she helped the Crone with the physical setup), and "Crone" (she guided the entire ceremony according to the plan that was cocreated).

The first time I celebrated with PTWs we traveled out of the city into the Virginia countryside. It felt like heaven being on acres of fields and woods, and I willingly helped the Maiden prepare the ritual site by shoveling out "cow pies," not without a few jokes, of course! The Crone guided us through an exciting rite that night that included the burning of branches representing patriarchal forces and fire leaping, which soon became an exhibition of great athletic prowess. The next morning, the sweet and healing Nymph woke us individually by offering a cool, wet cloth to refresh us.

Radical Paradigms

Through the process of co-creating our rituals and rotating all the tasks, each of us gained experience in all aspects of group rites. Members were empowered, instead of required, to follow the ways of a charismatic leader. This collaborative, nonhierarchical way broke out of the religious patterns of millennia, and each of us thus became seeds for the Aquarian Age that is now unfolding.

In the DC women's movement, we were becoming aware of the interconnections between sexism, racism, capitalism, imperialism, environmental degradation, etc., and we gathered in consciousness-raising groups to learn how these systems were affecting us and how we might change them. Many of us saw patriarchy as the system underlying all other systems of oppression. Contemplating how humanity has reached the current level of corporate exploitation and the unraveling of the ecology, I have asked myself, what was it about patriarchy that caused it to be so destructive? My answer is: the subjugation of Nature and the paradigm of power-over relationships, where one person or class of persons can tell another person or class of persons what to do.

As a student of psychology, I have read the studies that show how ordinary students become sadistic when they are put in control of other students, how a normally kind person can act to administer electric shocks because they are being told to. We have all seen how sexual and mental abuse flourish in every aspect of patriarchal society. Humans seem to have a weak spot when it comes to being given power over another human being. The temptation to misuse power seems too great for the majority of us. Perhaps we are not genetically suited for patriarchy! Perhaps we are more suited for collaborative organizations that utilize consensus as the form of decision making.

In *The Empowerment Manual* (2011), Starhawk has written about the trend toward collaboration that has been emerging in many social change groups. I like to believe the ingredients of witchcraft, plus nonhierarchical, empowering, collaborative group process, was a spell. It beamed this new paradigm deep into participants' individual selves and out into the collective unconscious. This beam implanted a Lightseed that is now sprouting in progressive communities. (PTWs planted only one of many Lightseeds of those revolutionary years.)

Speaking of group dynamics, my memories of PTWs are remarkably conflict free. The only issue that caused schisms in our consensus reality was whether to remain an open group or to close it. Some of us were all about openness and "the more the merrier," but others enjoyed the trust that builds when the same people meet together over time. The point was made that the delicate process of developing psychic perception in a society that ridicules such things might be most effectively accomplished among a group that is comfortable with each other, where mutual respect has been demonstrated, etc. I believe we resolved this conflict between openness to the new and comfort of the familiar by closing the coven to new members for certain periods of time or by having some gatherings where new people were not allowed to participate. This compromise seemed to work.

The Naked Truth About Our Rituals

PTWs also had the custom of celebrating naked. To reveal my nakedness the first time required courage, but within a minute or two of joining a circle of other naked women, I quickly relaxed and learned about the uniqueness of women's bodies. Immediately, I understood that the typical stereotype of women's beauty is an artificial creation that has little to do with the reality of our bodies. Not wearing clothes also contributes to a sense of equality, as people are not dressing up and using costume to wield influence and create status. On a spiritual level, nakedness allowed our energies to flow freely, and the power of our rituals increased accordingly.

Part of every ritual involved "raising energy" for our Magickal Working. We might sing songs/chants, rattle, use various percussion instruments, and/or dance. This was not a performance; expertise was not required. Rather, it was an exploration on the part of each woman to trust her innate rhythm, to listen, and to add her beat or voice to the whole. This also encouraged a sense of equality. I experienced the greatest transcendence when we stood close, our hands at the napes of one another's necks, and made freeform sounds (humming, chanting, animal sounds, whatever!), gradually building to a crescendo, cocreating a cone of power that we released to empower the intention behind our work. I felt it was like making love, a sensitive interaction among us that built to that cathartic release at the end. But no, in case you were wondering, we never performed a Great Rite (ritual group sex) together—at least not while I was there, and I have not heard of it ever happening.

As with many other groups in the women's spirituality movement that arose from within the second wave of feminism, we did not follow a strict liturgy passed down through generations. We were inspired by the writings and research of many, but especially by Z Budapest and her book on the women-only Dianic Tradition, *The Feminist Book of Lights and Shadows* (1974).[2] A genetic witch, Z founded the first known feminist witch's coven in LA in the early 1970s. We were also inspired by the writings of Shakti Gawain and her book *Creative Visualization*.

The Secret Revealed

I imagine you are curious as to the meaning of our mysterious name, "PTWs." The name was a secret known only to initiates in the circle, but we have agreed that it can be revealed now. It means "Pussy Tit Willows," a funny and celebratory name based on a plant and its resemblance to women's anatomy. PTWs was a funny group. Mischievousness was part of every ritual, thus fulfilling the *Charge of the Goddess*, "Let my worship be within the heart that rejoices, for behold, all acts of love and pleasure are my rituals. Therefore, let there be beauty and strength, power and

---

2 Luna Publications, 1974, revised and reissued as *The Holy Book of Women's Mysteries, Part 1* (first published 1979).

compassion, honor and humility, mirth and reverence within you" (Doreen Valiente Foundation). We had all that. And, I may argue, we were ahead of our time, predating the contemporary feminist movement with its "Pussy Riot" and the pink pussy hats of the women's marches that occurred the day after the inauguration of our 45th president!

The call of the countryside drew me out of DC in the early 1980s, and I could not celebrate with PTWs in DC anymore. However, I took all I learned with me into Spiral Grove, which I founded with the help of a small group in Rappahannock County, VA (just over the hill from where I had first celebrated with PTWs). Living in a rural area, I had to let go of my separatism if I was to find a group to celebrate with, and so the Grove was open to men. It has since become a 501(c)(3) Interpath Community of Nature Spirituality that seeks to promote equality, diversity, and harmony with nature. I embraced the archetype of Priestess for my life vocation, taking vows of service to the Goddess, but I have refused to be called a High Priestess and have worked to empower those with whom I celebrate. We have ordained many priestesses and priests in Spiral Grove.

Fireleaper, Summer Solstice, 1979

I rode the second wave of feminism and found my vocation through my experience with a lesbian-feminist coven in Washington, DC. Being a Witch/Priestess encompasses my spirituality and my environmental activism. I am dedicated to learning and sharing Goddess wisdom through an egalitarian process of circles celebrating the Wheel of the Year. My relationship with the Goddess evolves and ever deepens, but at its core is all that I learned through my first coven. I believe the principles I learned there are critical root ideas to be taken into the next age that is dawning as this current incarnation of patriarchal civilization breaks down. Blessed Be! I give thanks!

SHAMANISM AND FEMINIST SPIRITUALITY
Kim Duckett, from an Interview with Rose Norman[1]

We are a fierce and loving People.
We honor Femaleness.
Our religion is the Wheel.
Our language is Ritual.
Our Tribe: Goddess, Dianic, Amazon.[2]

Photo by Annette Lytle

Kim Duckett in ritual

My whole life has been about women and feminism. I taught women's studies in various western North Carolina universities for over thirty years. I began my vocation as a Teacher/Priestess in Dianic Goddess traditions in the early 1990s and was officially ordained in 1999. I received my PhD from the Union Institute and University in women's studies/feminist theory/Goddess spirituality, women's psychology, and transpersonal psychologies.

For me, during the backlash of the 1980s, women's spirituality *was* the women's liberation movement. It was always radical. For

---

1 Rose Norman interviewed Kim Duckett at her Asheville home July 10, 2015. Parts of this interview were used in Sasha Ray's "Finding Sheville," *Sinister Wisdom* 109 (Summer 2018): 120–25. This present story draws on additional material from interview notes.

2 Quoted from http://www.kimduckett.org/

me, it was never namby pamby, because whatever I was doing, I always had and applied my background as a radical lesbian-feminist. I never came into women's spirituality as a flowing gown kind of thing. I do feel that spirit, the Goddess, moved me in the direction of doing a PhD in women's studies and women's spirituality, so those two would always be combined with all that I knew and lived of radical feminism.

During the years of my PhD, I began a nonprofit organization called WHISPER (Women' Holy Inspirational Spiritual Performances, Events, and Rituals). I could do anything under the auspices of that nonprofit educational and religious organization, using their system to do my subversive work. It still exists and is how I still do my work.

I began a "Mystery School," and started teaching the "Women's Spiritual Journeys" class in 1993. It is a sixteen-week course that walks women through ancient Goddess cultures, and their loss, the Burning Times, and then information about all kinds of women's spiritualties in different cultures. I teach non-appropriation. So many white women think they do not have an earth-based tradition.

The first year of the Mystery School is the Wheel of the Year, taught as a spiritual psychology. It's different from other spiritual practices. For example, I would go to other people's Spring Equinoxes, and we would have our flower headdresses, and it seemed frivolous to me. It never touched me. Then I realized that at Spring Equinox we were talking about girls, and I began to apply all I knew about girls from women's studies, and that is how I teach it. Girls have really hard lives. I teach the truth about incest, the truth about stereotypes, and then maybe we'll get to the flower headdresses later.

My awareness of shamanism began in the early '90s. I had been taught that psychology didn't exist before it was begun by a white man in the mid-1800s. What, I asked my professor, and myself, were people doing before then? All roads led to shamanism, which, though now seen as the earliest religion, because of the continued separation between spirituality and psychology, is not always recognized as the first psychology. I studied other indigenous female shamanisms. I began to suspect that the Wheel we already had been following as a part of European pagan spirituality was a remnant of an ancient Old European shamanic tradition.

I have chosen to work specifically with European earth-based traditions such as the Wheel to offer women, and particularly women of white European ancestry and backgrounds, an opportunity to explore and find their own indigenous, earth-based roots and shamanic traditions rather than taking the spiritual traditions of others.

Sadly, at this time, the names that my foremothers of Old Europe gave to the women who embodied what is today known as shamanism have been lost. Although the full extent of their practices remains unclear, this situation is being rectified today by the work of Max Dashu, Vicki Noble, Barbara Tedlock, and others. I use the term *shaman* and practice shamanic methods with respect and care. As a feminist I take care to try not to appropriate the spiritual traditions of cultures other than my own.

The Wheel of the Year itself (I teach it both as a spirituality and a psychology) is shamanic in a number of ways. Across cultures, shamanic methods include the following: it incorporates a notion of the birth/death/rebirth cycle, it is used for healing/wholeness, and it includes the notion of crossing dimensions of reality to bring healing to this reality or another.

In January 2005, a big change happened in my life as a Teacher/Priestess. My board of directors trashed me, and after thirteen years, I no longer had a temple. I wrote about it in a chapter of *Stepping into Ourselves*.[3] Trashing behooves patriarchy. When I

---

3   Kim Duckett, "As Within, So Without: Some Psychological Aspects of Priestessing," in *Stepping into Ourselves: An Anthology of Writings on Priestesses*, ed. Anne Key and Candace Kant (Las Vegas: Goddess Ink, Ltd., 2014), 408–22. The section about trashing cites Jo Freeman's 1976 essay "Trashing: The Dark Side of Sisterhood."

contacted Jade, the head of the Reformed Congregation of the Goddess-International, which WHISPER was a part of, she asked me: "Was it power, sex, or money?" I said all three!-

My work now, and for the last twenty-seven years, has been to teach the Wheel of the Year as a psychology for women. I am still a radical lesbian-feminist, and this is the way I'm doing my work now, keeping opportunities for women to circle and teaching them enough that they become politicized. I became politicized around rape. You give women enough information, and if it's good information, women will wake up.

ELLEN SPANGLER AND STARCREST

Rose Norman

The first women's spirituality conference in the United States was held in Boston in April 1976[1] with many notable lesbians participating. Mary Daly spoke on "The Breakthrough from Phallocracy to Feminist Time-Space." Z Budapest gave a slideshow on "Politics of Spirituality and Herstory of Goddess Worship." Kay Gardner performed and gave a workshop on "The Dance of Life: Music and Movement." There were workshops by astrologers, healers, witches, and various kinds of Goddess worshippers. At the end, they encouraged everyone to go home and start their own women's circles.

That's exactly what Ellen Spangler did. She and two friends had driven to Boston from Jacksonville, FL, where Spangler had been instrumental in founding a domestic violence shelter, divorced an abusive husband, and changed her last name to protect her four children after she came out publicly as a lesbian. The Jacksonville women were powerfully moved by the conference and began doing New Moon circles out in the country with about two dozen women. Spangler became their leader, though she never saw herself that way and always sought group planning: "We started reading everything we could get our hands on and creating our own rituals. It was so touching. It filled my spirit. It wasn't any one of us that was the preacher. People were bringing what they could find, and we'd try it, and change things, discard things."[2]

---

1 The program for "Through the Looking Glass" is online here: https://jwa.org/sites/default/files/jwa032c.pdf.

2 Quotations are from my interviews with Ellen Spangler at Alapine on November 29, 2016, and September 29, 2019, and with both Ellen Spangler and Mary Alice Stout, again at Alapine, on February 29, 2020. We also recorded a Zoom follow-up interview on June 23, 2020. All of these will be archived at the Sallie Bingham Center for Women's History and Culture at Duke University.

The Boston conference had emphasized that women should be creative in planning their circles and not think there was only one right way. From that conference, she had learned "to bring things from the heart and promote healing on all levels of yourselves and of others and the world." Healing became a central part of her spiritual practice.

Spangler's spiritual quest took her to the Pagoda, a lesbian intentional community and cultural center in St. Augustine (near Jacksonville), where she participated in women's circles, and where she and her then-partner were croned at winter solstice December 1983, the first croning at the Pagoda. She also attended a psychic workshop at the Pagoda (probably February 1983), led by Kay Mora (1928–2003), a professional psychic who frequently worked with Pagoda women and who built a beachfront house adjacent to the Pagoda. From Kay Mora, she learned to go into trance and to safely channel a spirit guide that appeared to her as a Native American woman dressed in rainbow colors, the colors of the seven chakras. The women's circles that Spangler practiced were not strictly Native American or Wiccan, but drew on many traditions, much as the Pagoda rituals did. She saw herself as a healer on a spiritual quest and read widely in literature of spirituality.

In the mid-1980s, she moved to South Carolina, buying a five-acre lot in the country near Clemson University, next to friends who had a goat farm. Starting the healing and teaching center known as the Starcrest Holistic Healing Center was not her initial intent:

> When I got up there, I didn't know what I was going to do other than develop the land. I had bought an old house and moved it onto the land, and rewired and plumbed and repaired it, to have a home. I had been traveling and spending time with some Native American women, and I was sharing some of what I had learned with the South Carolina friends, about hands-on healing, healing our hearts in a sense, and

a different way of looking at spirituality. They suggested I teach a class about it. I had not done that before and didn't know how to go about it. How would I let anybody know? They told me about an alternative bookstore in Anderson, SC, nearby, where I could put up a flyer.

Soon, Spangler was regularly teaching classes that her students called Psychic 101 and Psychic 102, and had a mailing list of 400 people. She added a classroom to that old house to accommodate them. Women who took her classes began forming women's gatherings for ritual: "Two of them were Methodist ministers, who quietly (and unbeknownst to their church) joined the planning committee for the women's spirituality circles we had eight times a year: at the equinoxes and solstices, and the cross-quarter days (Candlemas, Beltane, Lammas, Hallowmas)." Gatherings drew up to fifty women from many different religious backgrounds, and they were particularly interested in Native American teachings.

In 1988 or '89, Spangler had been permitted to participate in a Native American women's sun dance in Arizona, one of whose directors was Beverly Little Thunder, with whom she later became friends. It was on the way back from an Arizona trip that she met Mary Alice Stout, who would leave a successful career in education to follow Spangler to South Carolina and become part of her journey for the rest of their lives.

While South Carolina was at least as conservative politically as Jacksonville, FL, Spangler actually found it easier to pursue her spiritual interests in a rural area where like-minded people seemed to find each other. A Clemson University religion professor attended the women's gatherings at Starcrest and trusted Spangler enough to ask her to cover two of her classes while she was away at a conference. The professor particularly wanted Spangler to talk to the students about the word "ritual," which they regarded with suspicion until Spangler helped them see how ritual is part of life.

Always especially drawn to Native American teachings, Spangler became close friends with a Cherokee police officer in Anderson who was secretly a shaman:

> He shared with me a lot of Native teachings that were really helpful and fit right in with the things that women were creating with spirituality. He emphasized what I had read from other indigenous people that what we refer to as God, that power, is much more than a person of any kind, but it's there for animals and plants. We all work together. It's not controlling anything.

That shaman showed them how to build a circle for ritual, with a large stone at each of the four directions, a particular kind of stone at each. They had chosen these stones intuitively for each direction, and later learned that they had picked the right ones according to Cherokee tradition. Something like that happened again when Beverly Little Thunder visited Starcrest and showed them how to set up a sweat lodge very strictly according to Native practices. Again, they had already set up things in a way that turned out to fit the Native way. Little Thunder, a two-spirit Lakota Elder from Standing Rock, ND (now living in Vermont), was amused by the granite and marble they had scavenged from a Georgia monument scrap pile, some of which were pink triangles. Little Thunder had been quite standoffish and skeptical when they first met at that Arizona sun dance, but over time, Spangler says, "she had gotten to know me and trusted my intent and my ability to run a sweat lodge and be honest with their concepts of it." Little Thunder participated in several Starcrest sweat lodges and also gave Spangler permission to do a pipe ceremony, a very great honor.

In the 1990s, Spangler and Mary Alice Stout learned about Alapine, a women's intentional community that friends from Pagoda were starting in the mountains near Mentone, AL. Spangler had been reading about earth-sheltered houses since the 1950s and had recently read a new book giving detailed instructions for building one. Alapine provided an opportunity to build that house with their own hands. Spangler was very skilled in construction and had done all the wiring and plumbing for the South Carolina house. So in 1997, when Spangler was sixty-three and Stout was fifty-two, they sold the South Carolina property and drove their van to Alapine, where they built a pole barn to live in while they built the earth-sheltered house they would call Owl Song.[3] At Alapine they continue to hold women's circles, including women from the larger community, often meeting at the Alapine community house.

Beverly Little Thunder with Ellen Spangler at Alapine

The South Carolina group continued to have sweat lodges for some time at the Starcrest location, and then moved them to another location nearby. Spangler keeps in touch with the people doing sweat lodges and reported that Beverly Little Thunder contin-

---

[3] Jessey Ina-Lee interviews them at their Alapine home in her video documentary series, the Landyke & Lesbian Documentary Media Project, 2005. These were at one time available through Woman, Earth, and Spirit, publishers of *Maize*, PO Box 130, Serafina, NM, 97569. https://womanearthandspirit.org/projects-1

ues to attend them, and that the woman who continued the sweat lodges in South Carolina also regularly assists Little Thunder with sweat lodges in Vermont. The women's spirituality gatherings continued for some time at other locations. Back in 1991, some of the women who had participated in women's gatherings at Starcrest had started an all-lesbian Wiccan coven, the Web circle, so for a time there was a Wiccan and a non-Wiccan gathering. Carol Creech, one of the founders of the Web women, writes: "Ellen was reaching a much broader audience of women who wanted to celebrate their connection to the Earth and would have cringed at calling themselves Witches. We were trying to do magic to change the patriarchy. Didn't always work too well, but we did some great magic!"[4] The Web circle lasted about twenty-six years, over time involving some twenty to twenty-five participants, some becoming initiated as priestesses. They celebrated their last Samhain in 2017.

Rebecca Alexander as Lucina at a Starcrest winter solstice gathering, December 1990. Rebecca and her life partner (now spouse) Carol Creech were still members of the Metropolitan Community Church in Greenville, SC, at that time, but went on to study Wicca and start a Wiccan circle in 1991.

Photo by Carol Creech, used with permission

---

4 Quoted from an email from Carol Creech to Barbara Ester, May 13, 2020. Used with permission. Carol Creech also cofounded the Upstate Women's Community in 1986, a lesbian group that had its first gathering at Starcrest. Carol Creech provided further information about the Wiccan group in email to Rose Norman 6-25-20. See also Beth York, "Lesbians in Upstate South Carolina 1986-2002: The Upstate Women's Community Newsletter," *Sinister Wisdom* 93 (Summer 2014): 114–18.

A CRONING ON WOMEN'S LAND
Kathleen "Corky" Culver

Gainesville, FL, got the idea for cronings from Z Budapest, from her books and from her visit to Gainesville in 1981. We got it and embraced it with a bear hug, expanding cronings beyond practicing pagans to giant community celebrations. Now it has spread worldwide and is used in increasingly mainstream circles. Back in the beginning, as with many of the feminist advances, lesbians were in the forefront. Our attention focused on women, and we had no husbands at home to worry about alienating with our new ideas that could undermine their patriarchal habits and privileges. We had only our own internalized assumptions to work through, such as the expectation that while an old man could be honored, being an old woman was the worst, done, over.

One writer who helped us was Mary Daly, who had just published a book overturning a lot of the anti-woman ideas embedded in the language. She saw the damaging words in a new light. With words like *spinster*, *hag*, *dyke*, *witch*, among the redeemed was *crone*.

Yes. And many of us were looking toward our own aging, as some of us were beginning menopause. Rather than accepting the denigrating, soul-sucking views of old women in patriarchy, we wanted energizing, inspiring praise and celebration, and we decided a ceremony of croning would be just the thing. We chose fifty as the age when this could happen, or any year thereafter. Fifty was about as old as any of us were. (That seems young now!)

So, here in Gainesville we began with spectacularly joyous cronings for Nancy Breeze, Gerry Green, and Jan Hahn, and in 1989 it became time for mine. I was living in a hand-built house on women's land and wanted my croning to be outside, among deer mosses and the wild. No! roared friends. What if it storms? Our land had no large indoor space. We were mostly living on from three to six thousand dollars a year, which meant renting a pavilion wasn't an option. I thought, well, why not string up a tarp, and that's what we did, a huge inelegant blue tarp, not the stuff of a garden party in the English novels I fancied, but just right for the rustic us.

Of course, it would be a potluck. I mean, what else could it have been? And there would be homegrown back porch string band music jamming, with cacophony and harmony in equal measures.

The daylong event would include a circle because we had rediscovered a pagan reverence for nature and seasons as part of our spirituality.

Exes flew in for the occasion—Donna, Randi. Barbara Ester and Vogel, along with Bonnie, drove up from the Keys. Bonnie made me a short cotton night robe, which I popped right into as a special outfit, topped with a witch's cone. Friends had found unpublished poems of mine, which to my delight they performed with grace and gusto. Shirley was hired to make a video.[1] There was a Lorelei cake. Lynda Lou and Judy made a frame for a weaving to which everyone contributed scraps of material, T-shirts; even a goddess statue was woven into the handspun wool. The weaving grew throughout the day.

By circle time, the rumor was that 120 women had flowed through. That's probably an embellishment of legend.

Flash Silvermoon called the corners, and each woman gave me a wish and a story or an original poem. How I wish now I had those on tape. I remember some—encouragement to write, a few mentioned they were amazed at how many old girlfriends were there, some told how meeting me and my friends had opened their lives. When my girlfriend at that time quite sincerely offered the wish for monogamy, everyone cracked up; she was right, though. All in good fun. While I don't remember many specifics, what I do

---

1 Shirley Lasseter's video of this croning, and many other events, is now archived with the Lesbian Home Movie Project, lesbianhomemovieproject.org.

remember was a feeling that my physical heart was being lovingly touched, tapped, punched, massaged. I can't think of how to say it. I felt the words and hugs were making their way into my chest and would be part of my being and strength for the rest of my life.

And that has come true. The croning is a time I can look back on when I need an attitude adjustment. These much-loved ceremonies have continued to this day. The cronings energized me and our community to make older years and retirement an "entirement," a "rewirement." Cronings celebrate the life so far and the fabulous crone years to come. Long live all crones! Long may we thrive.

FROM CONVENT TO COVEN... AND BEYOND
Sage Morse

What took me to the convent is hardly a noble reason: the idea had haunted me for over a year, so I went to prove to myself that I did not belong there. My high school classmates had bet me $50 that I would not last six months, so every time it began to feel too hard, I reminded myself that I was not going to lose that bet (I never did collect on it).

A little backtracking here: I ended up in a Catholic school in the first grade because public schools were teaching sight-reading, and my mother wanted me to learn phonics. Her partner was Catholic and pulled strings to get me in to her parish school. I was so out of place. I was an only child, not a Catholic, and my mother was divorced and living with another woman. In the sixty years that I knew her, my mother never admitted that she and Nan were lovers, or lesbians. Only after her death did Nan come out to me. At the end of the first grade, I decided I wanted to become Catholic, despite the fact that even at that age I had issues—that particular one was that I didn't believe in Limbo. I decided I could be Catholic and not believe in everything I was being taught. I went to the same coed school from first through twelfth grades, with the same group of kids all the way through.

I was never very pious, and really had no clue what it meant to be a spiritual person. I was academic, intellectual. I devoured Martin Buber, Teilhard de Chardin, the Vatican II papers. I understood more about communing with rocks (as per Chardin) than I did the Transubstantiation.

Chanting the prayers four times a day, in Latin of course, actually became the highlights of every day. On some level, one could almost go into another universe: I was at once part of a community and immersed in my own prayer. If for some reason

I had to miss a particular prayer time, I still knew that the prayer was occurring—not only at the Motherhouse, but in every convent of the order, a thousand women united in voice from Michigan (where I was) to New Mexico to California to Peru. It was both powerful and comforting.

So I stayed—for nine years. I discovered: depths I didn't know I had, a deep appreciation for ritual, a talent for organizing, a love for the Dominican way of life. I learned: science, theology, philosophy, how to identify birds and rocks. Most astonishing of all, I turned out to be a really good teacher.

The night of my twenty-third birthday, my principal, Sr. J., slipped into my bed, and we made love. She was not my first lover; the first had also been a principal of one of our schools. We had, of course, been warned about such alliances in the novitiate—the euphemism was "particular friends" since no one was bold enough to use the term *lesbian*. I told my best friend, another Sister, who could only say, "She'll hurt you as Sr. B.A. (my first lover) did, then discard you." She did, two and a half years later, but that is a story for another time.

The last two years were full of internal conflict. The day after I graduated from college with a Bachelor of Science, the prioress (elected head of the community) asked to see me in her office. I assumed it was to go over the plans for our Final Profession ceremony in which my class would take our final vows, and of which I was in charge. I was in shock when she told me that I would not be taking finals with my class as one councilor had cast a black ball against me.[1] (The councilors were four women elected by the community, who, with the prioress, ran it.) The reason she gave was that in her opinion the emotional support I seemed to need would best be found in marriage to a man. I knew what was

---

1 Historical note: The custom of "blackballing" a person was a medieval monastic custom. When it was time for a person to take final vows, they were voted on by a group of monks or nuns, using black and white balls. One black ball immediately dismissed that person from the community.

REALLY being said: "You are a lesbian and we know it." I was told if I wanted to renew for another year, and wanted to take finals the following summer, I would be accepted without another vote. That was an unheard-of concession.

At that time, any Sister who had graduated from college but did not have final vows went to the Institute of Theology to earn a Master of Theology. At the same time, in Michigan, a person needed to have a Master's in any subject except theology or P.E. in order to be principal of an accredited school. All of our Catholic schools were accredited. Just before Christmas, I got a letter from the Prioress asking if I had applied for a National Science Foundation grant to get my Master's in biology. With some bitterness, I wrote back reminding her I didn't have finals. She replied that she was aware of that, but she needed me to get my Master's and was directing me to do so. Grooming me to be a principal, and most of us knew that fully half of the principals had a female lover. It did make sense, since to act on one's lesbianism in that day took courage, strength, and a disregard for convention—all good attributes for successfully running a school.

I did not know if I wanted to remain in a community where one person could wield so much power for spurious, hypocritical reasons. Beyond that, I was beginning to have serious issues with the decrees of the Catholic Church regarding birth control and divorce. With a heavy heart, I said goodbye to the beloved life and rituals.

My extended family had had winter homes in the St. Petersburg, FL, area since the late 1800s. My mother actually got married in St. Petersburg and became pregnant with me there. Because she had already had two miscarriages, she went home to Michigan to have me. She stayed until 1971, when I moved her and Nan back to Florida. Even though I was teaching in many different places, Florida became my home base.

My introduction to myself as a witch was bizarre, at best. I was teaching at the finest college-prep school in the area, a private Episcopalian school in St. Petersburg. We rented space on a college campus, and my labs were on the opposite side of the campus from our main building. If it was raining, the headmaster sent a bus for my students so they didn't spend the rest of the day sitting in wet clothes in air conditioning. One day, no bus came. I called the headmaster, who said he had no bus available. "What," I demanded, "would you suggest I do about my students?" "Go out and tell it to stop raining," was his reply. Right, that would work. So to prove to him what an idiotic suggestion that was, I went out and told it to stop raining. It did. That totally startled me, but I put it down to coincidence. However, I tried it a few more times and it kept working—not with serious storms, but with rain and threatening weather. I connected with other witches, many of whom were healers. I was taken to several coven ceremonies, but found I was not comfortable with a mixed (male/female) group, or with the demand for perfect adherence to following a prescribed ritual.

Forty years after leaving the convent, I joined a coven seeking meaningful ritual and community with other witches but found the same discomfort. The ceremonies were stylized, planned, every detail, before we arrived, and we were told the order of events. I found I did not believe that magic, or spells, only work if one follows the ritual slavishly. I guess I have more faith in the power of the universe, and in intention.

For the last several years I have celebrated solstices, equinoxes, and other important days either as a solitary or with people I am close to spiritually. We have evolved our own rituals, and everyone contributes a part of themselves that enriches the rituals and makes them meaningful. For example, for one solstice one friend brought a plant for each person, and paper on which to write those things we wished to call to ourselves. We hung our intentions on the plant, so they could grow with the plant. Giving small gifts to one another, such as stones or shells, is now a part of some of our rituals.

As I studied rituals from many different religious practices, I have been struck by how many common elements there are. I do believe that ritual is important for us humans: maybe it centers us and reminds us of our connections to one another and to the earth herself. I look forward to each new celebration, knowing that each one deepens us and makes us aware of the gifts we have been given, as well as our obligations to make this world a better place for those who come after us.

Blessed Is and Blessed Be.

Left to right: Nan, Sage (then Sister Marie Theodore), and Sage's mother Isabel, on Profession Day, June 8, 1965. Nan and Isabel would be partners for fifty-three years.

MY JOURNEY TO THE DYKES OF DUNGENESS
Gail Reeder

The Dykes of Dungeness (DD) was an eclectic collection of witches from many backgrounds, each following her own path to spiritual enlightenment. Their paths converged for a year and a half around the circle of stones behind the Highland House for Wayward Girls in Inman Park, in Atlanta.

My path did not begin in Atlanta where the stone circle behind my house hosted the dancing witches. It began with my North Carolina grandmother. Her given name was Maggie, but everyone called her Mammy. She was the mother of nine, with generations of grandchildren. When I was young, I often spent time with her in the house her husband built. He added a room as each child was born until the house made a turn to the left to avoid the well. My mother, who grew up there, sent me to stay with Mammy when she needed a vacation from me. I admit I was not an easy child. Willful and given to fantasy, I did not always take direction well.

Grandmother took me to the Primitive Baptist Church on Sundays. It was my first coven experience. The hymns were chanted without accompaniment. The members of the congregation moved in unison, invoking a spiritual presence with song and prayer. Simple rituals like foot washings and the Lord's Supper were shared with reverence. Baptisms were in the Neuse River, for the church did not even have running water, much less a baptismal. The clean white robes of the saved ones were red with mud when they waded from the river, washed in the blood of the lamb. Sometimes in the chanting in the witches' circle I hear them still, singing and calling down the blessing of the spirits on those emerging from the water.

When the services ran long and I grew restless, Mammy sent me outside to wander in the graveyard beside the church. A playground of old graves and spirits with stories to tell was much more fun than the suck-back preacher who seemed to drone on forever. I sat on their chiseled stones and listened when they spoke to me.

Despite her dedication to the church, Mammy loved the devil's games, and we played cards on a three-legged table. One night she showed me how to call the spirits, and when she asked them questions the table would rock and answer. For years I thought it was a clever trick until I found out as a teenager that the table danced even when she wasn't around.

As a child I pored over pictures in geography books. Images of sacred spaces drew me in with their power. I longed to see the temples of Tibet and the vibrant greenness of Machu Picchu swallowed by the jungle. Stonehenge and the pyramids were favorite visitations in my imagination.

In college I took up tarot and found the cards hummed in my hands and seemed to be wiser than me. I continued to be sensitive to other worlds. I held a séance in old slaves' quarters for a documentary. The spirits did not show up that night, but I had seen them before when I slept in the old stone building.

When I moved to Atlanta in 1979, I found a restaurant just off Ponce de Leon called The Grove. It was a bohemian hideaway for artists and poets and witches. Sometimes the ghost of an old beatnik would wander through. A notice on a wall of messages brought me to my first formal circle with Lady Sintana of Ravenwood, who held traditional circles with both men and women. I bounced from there into a Wiccan-based class for novices and witch wannabes.

We practiced focusing and rituals, learned colors and chakras, practiced potions and spells and fire. There were lots of paths to take to reach the Goddess. We each braided our ritual belts with colored cords and purpose, saying a blessing with each twist. Mine was woven with happiness, fortune, and protection. It has served me well. Long after, I saw one like it by a Florida woman's altar and recognized a shared tradition. From that class came the circle of women who would become the core of DD: lesbians who wanted only to circle with other women, to worship the changing moon, and to celebrate the traditional witches' holy days.

We studied Wiccan and pagan religions. We came up with our own traditions and rituals. We all contributed pubic hair, which was used in the kiln by one of the witches who was a potter. A ceremonial drinking bowl with magical symbols and Goddess figures soon joined the rituals. We ate tiny cakes with menstrual blood baked in them to strengthen our bonds of sisterhood.

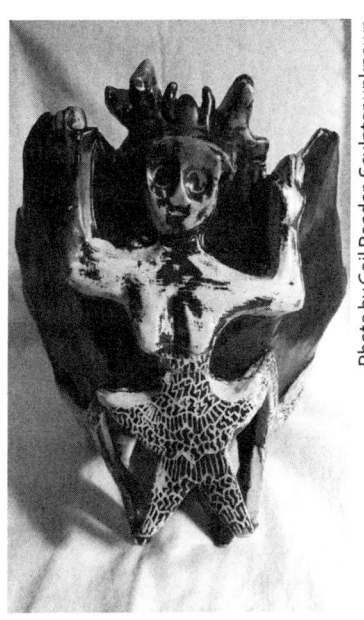

Photo by Gail Reeder. Sculptor unknown

Exterior of ceremonial drinking bowl.

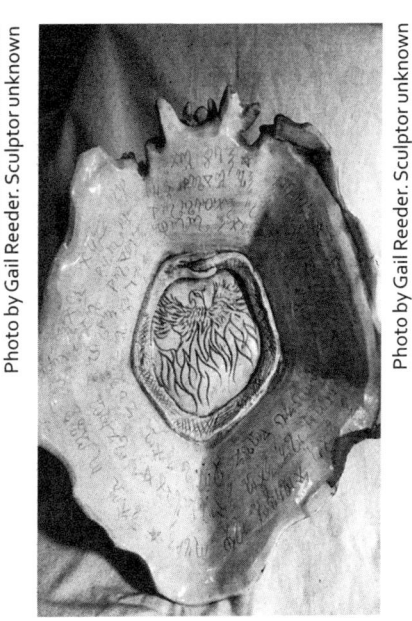

Photo by Gail Reeder. Sculptor unknown

Ceremonial drinking bowl. The interior reveals Atlanta's phoenix surrounded by the serpent's protective eternal circle.

Each of us took turns as high priestess, orchestrating the flow of the ritual. It was my night, and the fire blazed bright as we circled around in our long robes. Suddenly I sensed a presence behind me in the darkness. I turned to find a policeman with gun drawn, approaching the circle. I held up my hand and said, "Come no further into this sacred space." He replied, "I could not, my lady, if I would." And then he turned and disappeared into the darkness. I guess the neighbors had called 911 to report our firelit festivities.

Another night, Maria Dolan performed a ritual of her own. She always wore an old purple satin graduation robe for circling. That night she made a dramatic gesture to leave the old behind. She broke the empty wine bottle and began shredding her robe, cutting herself in the process. She seemed a madwoman with the broken bottle in her hand and her black eyes glistening in the firelight. The bloody robe was thrown into the fire. Good thing the police did not show up that night.

Highland House backed up against a vast open area. When the city tried to put a freeway through the neighborhood, we stopped it with demonstrations, but not before they had bulldozed a vast swath through Inman Park. The land lay empty and was covered with small shrubs and high grasses. On All Hallows' Eve we circled there, where the Carter Center now stands. Paths were trampled through the grasses, creating a labyrinth. On the way to the fire circle, witches stepped out of the darkness like ghosts, demanding our intentions. The veil between the worlds was traditionally thin that night, and the great power of that land took us truly out of time.

We went to St. George's Island where we rented a house and danced the spiral dance in the sand, sky clad in the moonlight. That was the date of the first or second Womonwrites, for Sarah Thorsen came late and missed the dancing, but she said it was worth it, because Womonwrites was even more wonderful than dancing naked by the ocean. I questioned her pronouncement, but later found out she was right. There were witches at Womonwrites, too, who also danced the spiral dance.

The Dykes of Dungeness shared many wonderful nights of rituals and celebrations. The stone circle was a place out of time, and we moved through centuries of traditions, honoring the lives of women past and present. How could it end?

It ended because of the very power and beauty that we created. The circling spiraled into new dances with new partners. There is a rule in some groups that its members will not date one another. Perhaps it would have saved the Dykes. The circle once so sacred and safe was full of tensions and anxiety. We no longer had the focus to raise the power of the Goddess.

When I left the circle, I took another path and did not look back. Nothing is forever and without change. Not even the Dykes of Dungeness.

Blessed be.

CHRISTIAN LESBIANS IN THE SOUTH

Judy L. McVey

Most lesbians raised in the South come from a background deeply influenced by the Christian church. Those values are strongly reflected in the family and community because the church has been at the center of their lives. Most were Baptist, Methodist, or nondenominational, and most of them were taught and preached a fundamentalist view of God, Christ, and the scriptures. In those earlier days, church was also the social event of the week, sandwiched between long hours of hard work in homes, businesses, and on farms.

Beyond attending church services there was Sunday School for all ages, and children may also have participated in training programs such as Baptist Training Union or Methodist Youth Fellowship. Wednesday night was church family night with supper, and in the summer, children usually went to Vacation Bible School. In the more rural areas signs are still on the highways—"Repent—the time is at hand!" or "Jesus Saves"—and prayers still take place at football games and the opening of most civic meetings. It is assumed that all are Christians—or certainly should be—and that all believe in God and the church. For people of color in the South, this is even more the case as the church has been their anchor and place of meeting from the days of slavery.

The South was a difficult place for a woman to come out, especially a teen, and especially in the more rural areas. The isolation was stark; there were few places of meeting except bars in larger cities. Many young lesbians just went through the motions of church to satisfy their family, hardly able to wait to escape. They were turned off by the church that told them over and over that God is mean and angry, women are second class, homosexuals are going to hell if they don't change. They rejected a spiritual life totally or found new ways of expressing and exploring their spirituality.

Others of us grew up participating in all church events and being part of some very real spiritual experiences within that framework, calling it getting saved, being born again, or finding Christ in the beauty and comfort of the liturgy. We definitely felt a personal encounter with God, possibly on a retreat or after hearing an inspiring speaker. Scripture, studies, and worship became truly meaningful to us.

Then we came out, realized we are lesbians. What should we do with that spiritual part of us that is real and meaningful? Many struggled with the negative messages from the pulpit and home and the very literal interpretations of scripture that told us we were condemned to hell. We fasted, prayed, agonized; we read and researched. There was no one to talk to. Were there others like ourselves?

I struggled with these issues myself, and my fervent prayers seemed to bounce off the ceiling. There were very few positive books available in the early '80s about Christianity and being gay. At that time, I was unable to see scripture through a wider lens, but it was more than a matter of dumping my constricting belief system. I had had an encounter with God and have had many more since. There was no arguing with that, but there seemed to be no place for me as a Christian lesbian.

In my earlier days I visited one of the Metropolitan Community Churches (MCC) in Atlanta. The first time I went, there were only men. A few years later I went back—there were six other women! I was so excited—and so were they to see me and my partner! That time we stayed, but we were aware that our experience as lesbians was very different from that of the men, kind and well-meaning as they were. So the women formed a support group that met in our house.

That first meeting we had around fifteen women present—they came out of the woodwork to meet as Christian lesbians in a comfortable and safe setting. The energy was high. We called ourselves the 2x4s because we met twice a month (two weeks out of four). We studied and discussed many topics and books, we took turns leading and shared with one another, we asked questions and searched for answers. We held a series of meetings at Candler School of Theology led by one of the seminary professors, a lesbian. The empowerment and spiritual growth we received from being in this group were tremendous.

An out lesbian Episcopal priest, upon moving to Atlanta in the '80s, was dismayed to find that her bishop would allow her to teach and preach, but not to celebrate Eucharist. She assisted in a small parish church under the care of a senior priest and was able to work with Integrity Atlanta. She and many other lesbians have chosen to stay in the church to address and work for change on issues such as women in leadership, inclusive language, negative and mostly male images of God, and a conservative interpretation of the Bible. Some of the more progressive denominations, such as the Episcopal Church and United Church of Christ, have moved in this direction and are now welcoming of diversity, including the LGBTQ community.

These churches are more often found in urban areas, however. In the rural Deep South, change is still slow. Fortunately, many more positive books may be found, science and biblical scholarship have made new discoveries, and the internet makes all of this available to us, wherever we live. Connie Tuttle, in her book *A Gracious Heresy*, describes the obstacles she encountered as an out lesbian in the Presbyterian church as she pursued an MDiv degree from Columbia Theological Seminary in Decatur, GA. When her denomination would not ordain her after graduation, she started Circle of Grace Community Church, an inclusive community of faith that is now meeting in Tucker.

Candace Chellew grew up in the Southern Baptist church in Buford, GA. Her father was the pastor, so church was her life from the time she was small. When she came out, she could not reconcile her new life with her church upbringing, so she dumped the church until her partner brought her to the 2x4 meetings. Candace was inspired to start "Whosoever," a monthly newsletter written for LGBT Christians to give them support for defending their faith against Christian fundamentalism. The title was taken from John 3:16 where Jesus said, "Whosoever believes in me shall have eternal life." The magazine went online and filled a tremendous need. The many questions and struggles that came across her desk from the readers led her to attend seminary at Candler School of Theology in Atlanta. After ordination she moved to Columbia, SC, with her partner, now wife. After some time there with MCC and the United Church of Christ, she started Jubilee! Circle, an intentional, progressive, inclusive community of faith. She also has authored a book in response to attacks from fundamentalist Christians, *Bullet-Proof Faith*.

Suzanne Snelling grew up in a United Methodist church in Decatur. As a child she was interested in "the raggedy man" who lived on the streets and wanted to come in to worship. Each time, he was quietly "managed" by an usher who would engage him in conversation to the side of the crowd and then, at the last minute, seat him in the back corner where he wouldn't cause offense. She wanted to talk to him and was always discouraged from it. When she was a teenager, she had an encounter with God—a gentle breeze and a certainty of God's presence, that peace that passes all understanding—while at Camp Glisson. When she later came out, her family told her she had to leave. Her church friends were uncomfortable and avoided her, so she quit going to her own church. She has a strong sense of identity as a Methodist, but the United Methodist Church, after twenty years of "study," voted to disallow gays and lesbians from their ordination process, so her church is closed to her.

She knows that she and the raggedy man are still not welcome in most churches. She has visited those that are open to gay people, but the structure, formality, pageantry, and politics put her off. She more easily finds God in nature, in the quiet of the out-of-doors. She is clear that God loves her and that her best response is to act toward others as Jesus taught us to be in the world. She demonstrates her faith by trying to follow Christ's teachings, loving people, and treating all with respect. She helps where she can with the individual needs of others and with volunteer work.

Many other lesbians experience their faith through personal retreats, contemplative prayer, or fellowship groups that meet regularly. They may attend less mainstream congregations, such as the Unitarian Universalist Church or Society of Friends, and they may borrow from other faith practices such as Christian yoga, meditation, tai chi, walking the labyrinth, and more. For many, God is most present in nature and a walk in the woods or an empty chapel. One woman says, "The church is inside of me." When there appeared to be no place of belonging, lesbian Christians found new ways of doing things. We have held on to our faith, questioned the parts that do not fit, and looked for other ways to share, learn, and worship.

CHRISTIANS, PAGANS, AND POLITICS: NOTES FOR A SPIRITUAL TIMELINE FROM *ATALANTA*

Lorraine Fontana

does the goddess live in southern amerika?

black lung
bible swamp
gospel choir
cherokee womon
and tropical shores
holy roller cotton picker
everglade seminole girl
turnip greens and creole gumbo
scarlett's curse and the abolitionists' fervor
moonshine and all the
madness, madness, madness
spoonbread, mint and
alligator carpetbagger
paddle wheel and lynching stump
white vested, fat politicians
or smooth talking/brimstone breathing men of god
revival tents and
sheets of terror
melungeon moonwomon
and bony weather strained Appalachian midwife
yes, our mountains are worn down but they are old
and look!
we southern wimmin insist that you see
beyond the smoky veil,
that the mountains in us are also wise,

they are fertile and
they rise in beauty.

>Marilynn
>*autumn, 1978*[1]
>(Nashville poet)

I write this as a founding, and "lifetime," member of the Atlanta Lesbian Feminist Alliance (ALFA, 1972–94). I write this after reviewing each monthly issue of the ALFA newsletter, later titled *Atalanta*, which started in September of 1973 and was published until our demise in 1994. I write this with any baggage that my childhood in a working-class, Italian, Catholic family in Queens, New York City, in a predominantly Catholic neighborhood, who never adopted another religious faith after I left the church but is currently a member of a philosophically based spiritual community (The First Existentialist Congregation of Atlanta, a Unitarian-Universalist Association member), might bring. I also write this as a seventy-five-year-old white woman, raised in the North, but who moved to the South at age twenty-one and eventually became a worker-owner at a metaphysical book wholesaler for twelve years (1986 to 1998), and was therefore exposed to many different spiritual traditions and practices during that time.

I say all that to add context, and to say that I don't claim objectivity, but some attempt at transparency. I started out to construct a timeline of activities and organizations related to religion or spirituality, and wound up tracking trends, developments, and inclinations of the ALFA (and Southern lesbian) communities' spiritual and religious interests and practices. These appear in over half of the published issues, 158 of 257 issues, not counting

---

[1] This is the second and last stanza of a poem titled "wimmin from down there," published in the ALFA newsletter in February 1979. Reprinted with permission from poet Marilynn Tucker.

repetitive information.[2] Most of them concern Christian-based or Goddess-based organizations, groups, or activities, with occasional references to Jewish activities. In these stories, the intersection of religion/spirituality and politics/social justice gradually emerges.

The very first reference to anything spiritual in the ALFA newsletter was in its second issue, September 1973, announcing a meeting of the Metropolitan Community Church (MCC), a "gay-friendly" Christian church founded in California in 1969. MCC first appeared in Atlanta in 1972, the same year ALFA was founded. MCC and ALFA were, in effect, the second and third out "gay" organizations in Atlanta, after the Georgia Gay Liberation Front, which was started in 1969. "Gay" was the umbrella term used back then until we dykes insisted that "lesbian" be added to the description of our queer community.

During the '70s and '80s here in the South, there was still an emphasis on women's relationship to Christianity and how patriarchal and homophobic Christian denominations were. Whereas MCC was nondenominational, there began to be queer-friendly church groups forming within specific denominations. In the November 1975 newsletter is a piece about "Integrity: a Gay Spiritual Forum" (Integrity was an Episcopal group), who were planning a special lesbian issue. Other gay-accepting Christian groups later formed, such as Dignity (Catholic) and Evangelicals Concerned. Affirmations, the gay and lesbian Mormon organization, had its annual national conference in Salt Lake City in 1986. About that time in Atlanta a new support group of "gay Presbyterian men and lesbians . . . began to share our religious heritage from our queer background." There was even an "Evangelical Outreach Ministries 6th Annual Celebration" in Atlanta with a guest speaker from the Church of God Gay Caucus (1983). In contrast to those churches in which LGBT folks

---

2 ALFA newsletters are part of the ALFA Periodical Collection at Duke University of about 800 grassroots newsletters and newspapers from all over the country, 1962–94.

had to form separate contrarian groups to demand, or beg for, acceptance, two Christian denominations in Atlanta existed from the 1970s who were "gay-friendly"—the Quakers/Friends and the Unitarian-Universalists.

In October 1977, an ALFA member who had been brought up in a Mennonite community jokingly formed "Iniquity: Shaker, Amish & Mennonite Gays," which met "every 1st Sunday down in the parking lot of the Little Five Points Zesto's." She then wrote about her experience growing up in that religious tradition and how she formed Iniquity at the Michigan Womyn's Music Festival that year: "It's not a 'real' organization. I guess part of what it represents to me is a fluid, expansive joke on a society which tells all of us, in every way it can think of, 'ok, be a lesbian! But you'll pay. You'll be cut off from everything else that matters to you. And divided into pieces.' To which we are learning—at our own pace, in our own ways—to answer 'Not if I can help it!' "

Some faith-based organizations like Clergy & Laity Concerned (CALC) were always about integrating their spiritual practice into their work for peace and justice. For example, Atlanta CALC had a workshop, "Personal Power & Peace," for those who wanted to be active in peace and justice work. I know myself that two denominations, starting in the '70s and '80s, and their Atlanta-based churches, were welcoming to queer people, and were always social justice–oriented: Unitarian Universalists[3] and the Quakers/Friends. The First Existentialist Church of Atlanta[4] was a UUA member. In the early '70s the Quaker House, as well as the "Big UU" church (UUCA), with its Sanctuary in-the-round, could always be counted on to host, and allow their space to be used for queer events.

---

3 The Unitarian Universalist Congregation of Atlanta and The First Existentialist Church [later Congregation] of Atlanta were UUA members.

4 They changed from Church to Congregation in 1989.

Signs of feminists seeking power and equity within organized religion appear in February 1974 when Murphy Davis (then a feminist seminary student, and later a key member of Open Door, the Catholic Worker Movement house in Atlanta) spoke on "Feminism and the Church" in relation to radical feminist theology. The discussion of, and writing on, feminism and religion was widespread during this time, as evidenced by a calendar announcement of a "Women and Religion" workshop in an Athens, GA, women's conference put on by W.O.M.E.N. (Women's Oppression Must End Now).

In June 1986 *Atalanta* announced that "Motlalepula Chabaku, a former South African ANC Women's League organizer," who was then a minister with the United Methodist Church currently living in Asheboro, NC, "will speak on the Spirituality of Black Women at the NBWHP" (National Black Women's Health Project) in the West End neighborhood of Atlanta. She was part of "Affirmations, the United Methodists for Women's and Gay Concerns" (interesting that they picked the same name as the Mormon LGBTQ-friendly group). That same year saw the holding of the Women's Ordination Conference, "an international grassroots movement of women and men committed to the ordination of Roman Catholic women." Mainstream religions all seemed to have their renegades, and/or internal challengers, both on gender and sexual orientation policy and belief. Samaritan College and MCC even attempted to form "the first accredited university with a gay and lesbian student body." They hired Ellen Ratner, the first person of Jewish faith to be appointed to Samaritan's Board. In October 1986 *Atalanta* advertised a gathering called "Woman-Church: Claiming Our Power," held to "explore ways of changing culturally engrained patterns of discrimination in religion as well as secular society." In June of 1988 the "2x4s" discussion group (started by two lesbian members of the All Saints MCC in Atlanta) formed to "try and reconcile being a Christian and being gay in a patriarchal society." It was open to all women and would later hold such discussions at the Cannon Chapel on the Emory University Campus and change their name to Christian Lesbians Uniting.

An October 1981 piece titled "The Judeo-Political Split" highlights what had already been, and would continue to be, unconscious Christian-centric lives within ALFA and the greater lesbian community that made our Jewish sisters' lives invisible and often set events on the same day as Jewish holidays. "Ignorance is a majority culture privilege, and unless ALFA wants to become an organization of white Christians and pagans, it is important to respect the differences among us." Here again we see the intersection of religion/spirituality and politics/social justice. For me, they always interact, and are reflections on each other. (See more stories about lesbian-feminist Judaism in this issue.)

During the 1980s, the Lesbian and Gay Interfaith Alliance continued its work against many isms within mainstream congregations, as queer kinship groups continued to form and operate within those denominations. Jewish members continued to thrive and to educate and challenge Christian and pagan sisters with celebrations of their own (e.g., Hannukah, December 1984), classes on Jewish holidays, customs and rituals, and making sure ALFA sisters knew the dates of important Jewish holidays. A Jewish lesbian group met the third Sunday of each month for a potluck brunch and discussion. Bet Haverim, Atlanta's synagogue for LGBT people, invited ALFA members to Shabbat services at the Quaker House.

References to Goddess churches began in October 1975, when *Atalanta* announced a defense fund for Z Budapest ("a woman practicing witchcraft in L.A."), who had been arrested under a law forbidding "fortune-telling." The Defense Committee was traveling the United States with a program of "dance, Goddess worship, women's spirituality and witchcraft," and wanted to come to Atlanta. Shortly thereafter, an ALFA sister put a bio of Z in the newsletter and asked if anyone else wanted to form a coven. That winter a solstice celebration happened at the ALFA House for the first time. In March of the next year, the first of a series about women's spirituality, goddess worship, and the prehistory of women's power appeared in the newsletter, with references to such books as Mary Daly's *Beyond God the Father* and John Allegro's *The Sacred Mushroom and the Cross*. The first women's circle at Sappho's Quarry (an old stone quarry east of Atlanta renamed by us) happened that Summer Solstice (1976), and the Snake Goddess of Ancient Crete was on the cover that September, which also had an announcement of "Witches Thanksgiving" at the ALFA House.

In May 1979 Daughters of the Earth held the Otter Creek Celebration of Wimmin's Spirituality near Louisville, KY, and for $26 you got a bed, workshops, vegetarian meals, and music by Linda Shear. That July a piece about the first Womonwrites conference featured this tidbit:

> Sunday breakfast was interrupted by the entrance of four ladies in sundresses, hats and gloves (Her Chorus from North Carolina), who treated us to a Sunday service unlike any other—beginning with the hymn "Life is Unfair This I Know, Jimmy Carter Tells Me So" and ending with a rousing chorus of "Glory, Glory, Dykes and Amazons," accompanied by a hand-clapping, foot-stomping audience.

And they still paint old lesbian-feminists as humorless?

By this time, well-established Wiccan covens, like the House of Ravenswood in Atlanta, were dividing into separate women's covens (e.g., the Amelia Earhart Coven) "combining Dianic and Celtic tradition and affirming the Goddess within ourselves and throughout the universe."

In January of 1980, ALFA received a letter from Susan Saxe, a lesbian member of the Weather Underground who had been on the FBI's Most Wanted list for five years after fleeing from a bank robbery in which one of her comrades killed a police officer. She had been captured and imprisoned for two years awaiting trial, then decided to plead guilty so she could serve time and get out to continue organizing. In her letter she was worrying about what she saw as the "tipping too far [of the lesbian movement] toward the cultural . . . that is going to be debilitating to us politically." Here "cultural" refers to the wider conflict within lesbian-feminist groups and circles about whether we should be building "women's culture" (an alternative cultural world for lesbians outside the patriarchal system) or fighting more directly to break that patriarchal system, and its institutions, through direct political action and organizing. Within ALFA there were women on both sides of this debate, and all places in between. But disagreement didn't stop the growing Goddess and Wiccan community. The March 1980 newsletter featured an ad for *Themis: The Voice of the Feminist Witch*, the newsletter of Z Budapest's Susan B. Anthony Coven No. 1 in Los Angeles.

All the while, the Atlanta MCC continued to exist and eventually was large enough to split into two separate MCC congregations, so Christian-centered lesbians, and other queers, continued to thrive. There was even a chapter of a Seventh Day Adventist group, SDA Kinship, formed in Bradenton, FL.

But the growth within ALFA was in earth-based religions, not Christian organizations. In December 1980, the cover of *Atalanta* was titled "Hallowmas," with an article about its meaning inside, as a Wiccan time of healing and ritual that later transformed into Halloween. Wiccan holy day celebrations continued that next year. Another ALFA member took to calling out religious fundamentalists in her new monthly column "Maria's Strictly Impartial Believe It or Else" and highlighting creative responses to homophobia, such as San Francisco's Sisters of Perpetual Indulgence. In July of 1981, Nancy and Ann Moonbow started another series of articles on witchcraft, and the newsletter advertised a national Goddess Rising Conference for March of 1982 in Sacramento, CA.

An August 1982 story signed by Artemis outlines a clear, sequential relationship between lesbian-feminism and Wicca:

> I am a Feminist, a Lesbian, and a Witch. Each of these represent a step in my life. The first step was learning that laws had been created that allow destruction and oppression of the land and her people, and I became political—I became a Feminist. The second step was when I saw that our culture sang songs celebrating womyn's isolation, and painted pictures of bondage and rape. I discovered the healing dignity in the love of womyn—I came out as a lesbian. The third step was when I grew to understand that for centuries the churches kept the fires burning in their reverence and worship of a patriarchal order that would deny womyn a voice and a vision—I emerged a witch.

Our quest for healing as lesbians began to focus on meditation as a spiritual practice. In October 1982, ALFA House hosted evenings of "Silent Space, Healing Place" for women to meditate and/or work with other women offering "healing energy." The ALFA member who organized it saw this as the first step in her vision of a "spiritual foundation [later called The Sanctum of Divine Daughters] that gives honor to the Daughters of the Earth." The following January, another member advertised a "trance group" to achieve expanded consciousness, and in July 1983 there was a "Rainbow Bridge" workshop "to stimulate and direct psychic/intuitive awareness in everyday life." That same year, a meditations ritual and support group studied Starhawk's newest book, *Dreaming the Dark*.

August 1983 also saw a celebration of thanksgiving at the ALFA House, the "LAMMAS Festival of Thanksgiving for the First Fruits of the Goddess." In October we had a "Phases of the Moon" workshop "in which we will magically experience the connection between our monthly bleeding and the moon." ALFA member Christina Ishtar wrote "Know Your Pagan Holidays" for the February 1984 newsletter, and that month's Candlemas (aka Groundhog Day) was celebrated. In April, Maya Smith, who had studied with Starhawk, presented a five-week series on "The Elements of Magic" for $50, and a follow-up four-week series, "Weaving the Circle Stronger," for $45. The cover of the May 1984 *Atalanta* featured a drawing of nude women cavorting in various ways in a circle around a fire pit, surely a coven celebration.

Art by Nancy Lynn Oswall

The *ALFA Newsletter* became *Atalanta* in January 1977. This cover from 1984 (Vol. 12, No. 5, 9984) features a drawing titled "The Circle."

In October of 1986 the "Earthwitches, a feminist ecologist collective," sponsored a trip to Sapelo/Cebretta Islands, on the Georgia coast, for wilderness camping to "reconnect with the Earth." In November, "Of a Like Mind, an International Network of Spiritual Women dedicated to bringing together women following positive paths to spiritual growth," advertised their quarterly newspaper available on a sliding scale. Early the next year there was a "Boogiewombin[5] Women's Week at Candler School of Theology" featuring Mary Daly, Nell Bringle, and Letty Russell.

ALFA couldn't be beat at combining fun and celebration with feminist spiritual and social justice concerns, as evidenced by

---

5 Boogiewomen, Boogiewimm, Boogiewombin. The name changed, but they were always the social event planning committee at ALFA.

the February 1988 "Chem-Free Venus Day Dance, a modern-day sock hop named in honor of Venus, the Roman Goddess of love and beauty, who preceded St. Valentine by centuries." Organizers created a safe space celebration where sober sisters might feel welcome and safe, held at the wheelchair-accessible and queer-friendly First Existentialist Church of Atlanta ("First E"), with tickets sold at Charis Books & More. The following year, Charis Books featured an evening with Julia Perilla-Parker and Kathie Hennessey, co-authors of "Dialogue on Spirituality," and shortly after an evening with storyteller Jay Goldspinner about her goddess tales.

I realize what a different time we live in today as I read this notice in the May 1989 *Atalanta*: "Holistic Herbalism, a weekend of Native American herbalism and spirituality taught by a Lakota Sioux medicine woman [no name given], herbalist and sundancer, in North Druid Hills in Atlanta," $65/day, $120/both days. In 1991, there is a "Wise Woman Tradition Apprenticeship week" in Asheville, with "Whitewolf, including herbs, wildercrafting, women's health, moonlodge, massage & magic." Our cultural appropriation antenna would immediately go up now, and questions would be asked to determine if these were really Native sisters or non-Indigenous women making money off of the appropriation and use of Native names, teachings/knowledge, ceremonies, and articles. I don't believe this is paranoia, but rather based on too many examples of such inappropriate use of Indigenous people's history, culture, and spiritual practice by non-Indigenous folks. In the March 1986 *Atalanta*, there was a serious presentation of a S.E. AIM (American Indian Movement) Conference resolution: "The Attack and Theft of Sacred Ceremonies & Articles," which condemned non-Native (usually white) people who were selling, commercially capitalizing on, sacred Native ceremonies and objects. This included women who wrote books, and held workshops and seminars, which combined Native American and women's spirituality. This, of course, holds true to the present day.

Another reminder that the trope that lesbian-feminists have no sense of humor is not true was Morgan Grey and Julia Penelope's *Found Goddesses*, reviewed in the May 1989 *Atalanta*. Here you will find "a listing of goddesses for the modern dyke to call upon. There is Asphalta, Goddess of Roads and Parking Spaces, Dea Ablea, Goddess of Fitness Chic, and Et Cetera, She-who-takes-much-for-granted."

By the end of the 1980s and beginning of the 1990s, it was not uncommon to see a Seventh Day Adventist lesbian and gay support group, next to the Fourth Annual Womyn & Witchcraft Conference, and a local Spring Equinox celebration with a discussion of metaphysics and meditation. A 1992 column called "Religious News" appeared in the newsletter, gathering all such info into one space. Also during this period, under the will-miracles-never-cease heading, is *Emerge!*, a periodical by Christian scientists supporting lesbians and gay men.

Two *Atalanta* stories from 1992 (two years before ALFA dissolved) show how closely linked spiritual and political concerns had become. In July, the Pagoda-temple of Love, in St. Augustine, FL, celebrated her fifteenth year as "a spiritual/cultural home and retreat/guest house for lesbians" by paying off the mortgage and embarking on a $30,000 renovation project to make Pagoda more wheelchair accessible. In October the "Woman's Alliance for Theology, Ethics & Ritual (WATER)" sought donations from Atlantans to "build a movement of people who want this country to be a just place, a healthy planet with healthy people whose dreams of equality are not just for their children, but for themselves."

Grandma Allie became ill several months later. She was taken to Mission Hospital in Asheville where strict quarantine orders were in place, and only family members were allowed to visit. We told the guard we had come to see our dying grandmother and got in. She opened her eyes and looked alert when we entered her room. She said, "I was waiting for you'uns. I knew you'd come." She died that day, but when the time she had seen came, her love for us was as alive as it had been in her living room years before.

Our first fall in the Blue Ridge, we had met another elderly couple at a tobacco handing. They seemed very interested in us although at that time we lived in another community. Our neighbors Merle and Cleophus said the old couple, Lyda and Ethel, had been "courting" us with their questions that evening. Months went by before we saw them again.

The following spring my lover's parents locked us out of the house while we were at work and put the land and home on the market. They even took the furniture. They may have thought we would give up and each return to our separate pre-Appalachian lives, but if so, they were wrong!

Staying with friends an hour away, we began house hunting. We found a place a few days later in a settlement near where we had lived. We didn't know that it was just down the hill from Lyda and Ethel, the couple we had met at the handing, until they showed up to visit. We apologized for not having porch chairs, offering them the swing and seating ourselves on footstools from the house.

They had heard what had happened. He spoke first, "You'uns must be feeling pretty sorry for yourselves, so we thought we'd come tell you about a hard time we had. I was raised right here in this house. When Mammy and me decided to marry, we started a log house up in the mountain—just twelve by twelve. It was already cold when we married and moved in."

She continued, "We got in bed and stayed awake too late. When we woke up, the fire was out and there wasn't any matches hen!" He took up, "We had to get on the mule and ride down to

APPALACHIAN QUILT MAGIC

Helen Renée Brawner

A quilt is generally three layers: a woven or pieced top; a batting center for warmth; and a woven back, held together with the layers sewn together. This quilt story's top is the acceptance of the first lesbian newcomers (and first known gay couple) in an Appalachian community. The batting is the winning of our neighbors' hearts as they won ours. The seldom seen backing is the doors we opened for others to follow.

In Madison County, NC, aka "The Jewel of the Blue Ridge," where Bonnie and I lived from 1972–78, our neighbors accepted us as part of their tiny settlement, some as family. We did not use the word *lesbian* to describe ourselves to these neighbors, some old enough to be our grandparents. They might not have understood the word, much less its social implications. Nevertheless, our relationship was accepted without criticism.

We first realized this with an elderly neighbor who had lived most of her life in our first home. "Grandma Allie" and husband "Pap Moody" had moved down the mountain near their son and daughter-in-law. We visited them regularly, listening to All' stories and enjoying the playful way they argued.

One day Moody was in the garden when we arrived. Allie she had hoped we would stop by that day. She had dreamed us and had something to say. We later shared that we fundamentalist condemnation at that moment. Instead s us she had seen us love each other more than most won love each other—that we were closer than sisters. Sh dreamed a time to come . . . a time, children, when you stay together. That will be painful for you'uns. I'll be want you to remember me and how much I love you w' comes. My love will be there for you then."

her mam and pap's to borrow fire. Everybody knew then that we'd slept till up in the day."

Ethel finished with, "We thought if we told you'uns about our hard time when we were first together, maybe you'uns wouldn't feel so bad. We're right up the hill if you'uns need anything."

They meant it! They taught us to get wood with the mule and a tractor and helped us adjust to the wood cookstove, the English cottage fireplaces, and the red clay of the garden. They watched for smoke coming from the chimneys in the morning, brought food when we were too sick to care for one another, loaned us a truck down payment when the VW blew up, and worked side by side with us on their projects and ours. They had been together nearly sixty years and still giggled and snuggled like teenagers. They said it was because each always made sure the other had whatever they wanted.

One February morning, after we had all pulled corn the whole day before, Ethel woke up sick. The ambulance came, but a clot had gone to her vital organs. She died that day but was put on life support. Lyda finally told them, "That's not Mammy anymore. Let her go on." After the funeral the children sold his mule, and he moved near Asheville with their son but was soon homesick, vowing to come home "after hog-killing time."

One day he drove home, then down to ask for help going through Ethel's quilts that a mouse had gotten into. Up at their house, he and I stood on either side of a trunk at the end of the bed, quietly lifting her colorful hand-stitched quilts one by one, unfolding, turning, then refolding each, making a pile of clean ones here, a pile of soiled ones there. Finally, breaking the silence after unfolding a nine-patch she had made of pastel flannels with pink rose-patterned flannel backing and border that the mouse had missed, I said, "If I was a mouse, I'd have slept in that one." He chuckled and nodded. I noticed that he put that quilt in another place. When finished, he asked to be alone while I walked home to tell Bonnie he would be down in a few minutes and wanted to talk to us both.

When he came in the door, the quilt was under his arm. He said, "Mammy always wanted to give you girls a quilt but was afraid she'd offend you'uns. I know she'd want you to have this, so I'm giving you this quilt on one condition." A slight smile began to form as he continued, "If you'uns ever stop sleeping together, you have to split it right down the middle!"

We had a good laugh at the time and said we would but, when we did "part ways" after six years, we could not keep our word. We spoke of taking turns. My turn was first, lasting decades.

The quilt traveled to campsites in North and South Carolina, Tennessee, and Georgia, and served as my Womonwrites bunk identifier for years while Bonnie recovered from a life-threatening illness and built a new life back in Florida with a new partner. Solace in times of grief and warmth without heaviness kept it a favored quilt for home, travel, or ritual.

As it softened and its binding grew frayed, elders of our former settlement disappeared from sight. The grandfatherly neighbor who had given the quilt on behalf of his recently departed wife sat down after lunch to rest before resuming the garden harvest and distribution he was well known for and simply fell painlessly into the deep sleep of death. Our neighbor Cleophus and another neighbor Loy, whom we had barely gotten to meet, were not so lucky. They and former landlord Howard succumbed to a fast leukemia common among tobacco farmers. Reba, who had lived across the garden and kept us entertained with tales of travel, love of wine or "Night Owl" (sold as Nyquil if nobody was going where wine could be purchased), and offers of marriage yelled from her porch "to the first man who shows up and can drive a nail," passed without our knowing the when or why. Pap Moody walked himself to death to and from Grandma Allie's grave for lack of his arguing partner of over sixty years.

A few of the young folk we had known also vanished from Madison County. Most, however, like us, changed partners or environs and kept right on living. Babies we had greeted grew to adulthood, and more grew alongside them. Madison County filled up to thickly settled, a destination for whitewater, old-time balladry, skiing, and retirement. Those who stayed and clung to the old ways kept their love of nature and of the time-honored Appalachian gift of gab.

That gift of gab was how the partner who had once shared the quilt first came to know that I was still alive. While she visited on Big Pine, a friend and former neighbor announced my graduation from a baccalareate nursing program. Her partner of decades responded sarcastically, "Well, I guess you want to rush right out and contact her!" and was answered, "No, not now." The seed was sown, unbeknownst to me.

Two turns of the wheel later, content with solitude and grandmother time, I had finished my bedtime regimen and turned out the light. Remembering an intention to look for a friend's health update, I turned the light on again. I found instead, after nearly thirty years of silence, a friend request from my first Bonnie.

Friending led to texting, then lunching and talking six hours face-to-face midway after a nearby morning clinic. Soon we picked wineberries, created jam and mozzarella, and made plans to go camping. Our choice was Cumberland Falls. Fireside meals, hikes, and night talks felt familiar. We kept a distance between us, reminding ourselves that we were getting to know one another after years living dissimilar lives, but discovered synchronicities in experience and choices. She was grieving a spouse of many years. I was grieving family members, close friends, and younger lovers also gone too soon. She had felt contacting me important for her healing. I realized that she was a catalyst for my own. We pledged to return to Cumberland Falls.

Home from Cumberland Falls only one day, we met halfway at midnight for the Perseids at Waterrock Knob on the Blue Ridge Parkway. We had dressed warmly, preparing for falling dew. We snuggled close together under meteor showers until cloud cover, then in the Subaru until dawn. We were no longer keeping our distance! Plans for Harvest Moon at Cumberland Falls began shaping up for a longer stay at "our campsite." I began looking for the quilt for us to sleep together under again as a surprise for "our" bed.

The quilt worked its magic! It was our bed in our home. The rain came, and with it the cool of early September nights. We stood in a misting rain for the ghostly moonbow, picked wildflowers for our table, flew a Woody Blue Terra-ist flag over our campsite, and gathered grapevines for baskets near the CCC overlook before heading home. The love and acceptance gifted us in soft pastels when we were very young lives on in the tangible reminder of a beloved nine-patch quilt and memories having come full circle.

Bonnie and Helen Renée with their quilt at Womonwrites, Fall 2015.

Photo by Rose Norman

WELLSPRINGS FESTIVALS, 1995-97
B. Leaf Cronewrite

I met the producer of Wellsprings, Debra Kaufman, back in 1977 in Memphis, TN, when I was coming out as a lesbian. She introduced me to lesbians who have become lifelong friends. She was often talking about women's land and women's gatherings through the years. In 1995 she called to say she had decided to create her own festival and hold it on her remote farmland in northwest Mississippi. She called it Wellsprings, counting on the creativity of women to be shared, "to spring up" through music, spoken word, and art. Deb met the Wellsprings logo designer Harriet Buckley, at Meristem feminist bookstore in Memphis. Harriet's idea was to create a double women's symbol with waves flowing from the arms above the word "Wellsprings." This green imprint was put on a beige T-shirt that many of us wore for all three Wellsprings festivals. My partner Drea and I made the eight-hour drive from Georgia each year. Being with old friends and meeting new ones to help create festival was always worth the drive.

Wellsprings logo designed by Harriet Buckley.

Deb had mowed her field with a big tractor and set up some big tents to gather under. Most of us who attended the first Wellsprings remember how unprepared we were for the cold that October night that we were huddled together under a big tent to listen to Mimi (now Mosa) Baczewska sing. Mosa's memory was of the cold, too, and of the many "sweet women" who attended. Some women pitched tents or slept in their trucks or vans for primitive overnight camping. Drea and I and a number of other women rented chilly rustic cabins at a nearby state park.

The atmosphere was free-spirited, women feeling they could be themselves in this remote area. Some women had even brought a huge hoop that framed giant bubbles that floated among the laughing women. We had a drum circle in a sunny field, my first time seeing so many women drummers. Around fifty women attended, and we talked, we sang, we ate, we were out and proud.

Yet some rural lesbians nearby feared they would be outed, and that their homophobic neighbors would retaliate. It was still a dangerous time to be identified as a lesbian. A city reporter from the *Memphis Flyer*, an alternative newspaper, sneaked into the festival and published the location of the lesbian gathering and pictures, writing an inflammatory piece insinuating that witches were present. There was no retaliation by the neighbors, but Deb decided the location would change the next year.

For the following two years, we all gathered for Wellsprings at Meeman-Shelby Forest State Park outside of Memphis. Many of us tented those years. We had choices of workshops during the day. Some of us sat in folding chairs in a circle outside and talked of building a lesbian nation, or played drums and got lost in the rhythms. Harriet Buckley led a workshop teaching us to create small drums. Other women created art projects. At night we had indoor facilities with a stage where women sang or read poetry or danced.

We often gathered in the chilly mornings or late evenings at the coffee and tea station set up under tents. We bought homemade treats from the Peanut Butter Café. As part of our registration, each woman selected a beige ceramic mug with a different animal sketched in blue. I still have mine, a zebra on one side (Drea has a fish) and Wellsprings in flowing script on the other side.

I have wonderful memories of a time when my very resourceful and determined friend Deb created a small lesbian festival that drew women from across the South to feel nurtured, creative, and safe.

Leaf, Gail Atkins, and Gwen Demeter enjoy coffee near the Peanut Butter Café. Leaf is wearing her Wellsprings T-shirt.

BECOMING A LESBIAN AT WELLSPRINGS FESTIVAL

Robin Toler

Much of my story about Wellsprings Festival is true, based on my experience. I know for certain that my attendance at this small Mississippi women's festival carved a deep emotional impact on me. I was a shy, naïve Southern woman, not fluent in women's issues. Hell, at thirty-four years old, I didn't know women had issues.

This would be my first women's festival ever. I was nervous and excited to get through preparations for attending: getting ready, gathering everything I would need to take, loading my vehicle, and coordinating my time of arrival—before we had cell phones or Internet access. I had a paper map showing where I was supposed to go— Memphis. I met my friend and her girlfriend there. We caravanned to a place near Holly Springs, MS. There was mystery around the festival's address; much was kept secret. I wasn't sure why, yet I didn't want to ask questions or seem ignorant. I was being submerged layer by layer into a secret society that was luminous and radiant, yet buried in darkness. It felt empowering.

When I pulled onto the land, I saw different women: Amazonian, tattooed, frail, young, old, large, from shapely femme to extra-large butch, dyke-like. They worked together synchronistically, building the stage, unpacking boxes, setting up spaces for workshops, rigging lights, unwrapping electrical cords and extension cords, assembling structures, setting up tables, coffee bars, chairs, and artist's niches for selling works and wares. I had rarely seen women working in earnest together. This was amazing.

And there were shoes and no shoes: army boots, motorcycle knee-high strapping boots, high heels, flip-flops, tennis shoes, gladiator sandals, feet with socks, and bare feet with mud and dust and everything in between. I was curious as to where these women were from. What were their stories? I was from Louisiana; some were from Tennessee, Mississippi, Georgia, Alabama, and North and South Carolina.

All the performers were incredible! A slender white woman from the northeast with delicate blue-green eyes practicing on a keyboard. A tall, thick African American guitar player composing love songs. A woman with wild, graying dreadlocks performing spontaneous movements of interpretive dance. Especially memorable was an African American woman playing the electronic saxophone under an indigo starlit sky. Her sharp, piercing sounds flew across the night like the northern lights in miniature, transformed into sound; I was carried into another realm. Something substantial was bubbling up from my inner being, transporting me.

Next morning, new sounds lured me out from where I slept. I walked, trance-like, following the beat of drums, moving toward the rhythm and the deep, reverberating sounds of drumming. I approached a large circle of women seated, pounding drums between their thighs. I was mesmerized by the sounds of booming drums and the sight of topless women. Once in the circle of women drummers, I felt transformed—I had become one of them.

Drum workshop. *Photo courtesy of B. Leaf Cronewrite*

CHOCOLATE CHEESECAKE

Barbara Esrig

Many of you readers have sampled what now has become my signature special-occasion dessert extraordinaire. But I wonder how many of you know the event that publicly christened it.

It was March of 1982, and some Gainesville lesbians rented the Hippodrome regional theatre for the sellout performances of Sallie Ann Harrison's *Turkey Baster*, a groundbreaking play about a woman coming back from California to tell her two lovers she was planning on self-inseminating with a turkey baster (this, by the way, wrecked their Thanksgiving). This play was followed by Linda Wilson's quite amazing original lesbian folk opera, *When We Dead Awaken*, the fabulous tale of an attempted rescue of Amelia Earhart by the Amazons.

For those of you who don't remember 1982, it was a time of transition. While the country's political tide, with Ronnie Reagan and his sidekick George Bush at the helm, so to speak, started its conservative turn to the right, we in the lesbian-feminist movement still had hopes that we could not only make a difference, but change the world. While the country was dealing with double-digit inflation, concern about the possible imminent demise of the "traditional" family, and Reagan proclaiming economic sanctions again Libya, our political concerns were in a different direction—primarily the legality of lesbian rights, the growing anti-abortion movement, and that supporters of the Equal Rights Amendment were unable to get enough states to ratify it, with the realization that the country was once more unwilling to guarantee women constitutional rights equal to those of men.

On the other hand, the feminist and peace movements were all over the media, and *media* was not a dirty word yet. TV shows like *All in the Family*, *Cagney and Lacy*, and *M*A*S*H* were still having first runs. At the Academy Awards that year, *Gandhi* won Best Picture and Meryl Streep won Best Actress for *Sophie's Choice*, a movie about a Nazi concentration camp. Womyn's music was explosive with Alix Dobkin, Tret Fure, Willie Tyson, and of course the Holy Trio: Holly Near, Cris Williamson, and Meg Christian in their prime. Across the country Take Back the Night marches were getting big press; womyn's clinics were continuing to model a new direction in health care. We had a vision, and we had the answers. Judy Chicago's *The Birth Project*, celebrating birth and creation, broke the iconographic silence (few known works in Western art dealt with the subject of birth up to that point), allowing womyn artists to represent womyn's experience. Some even saw parthenogenesis as a safe alternative to birth control!

I say this all to give you an idea of what the climate was, which brings us back to my recipe. So Linda called me up and asked if I would make several of my not-yet-famous chocolate cheesecakes to serve at the intermission, and I said sure, planning to try out my new food processor doing it.

A womon in the community and fellow foodophile, Cheryl Lamay, asked if she could come over and help with the afternoon's project. I didn't know Cheryl very well at that time and was surprised and delighted that she not only volunteered but was eager to help. Now food processors still had the aura of high tech for both of us, and after stuffing all the ingredients into the base, I turned it on, which proceeded to throw the top off. Chocolate cheesecake batter immediately whipped across the kitchen, landing on the walls, the ceiling, the floor, and all over us! We were stunned at first, and then nearly peed in our pants laughing so hard. And this, I might add, was one of those events that led to many more successful, less calamitous experiences in the kitchen with Cheryl. We always say that this was the bonding that brought our friendship together.

In case you're wondering, we did clean up the kitchen and made several cheesecakes, and they were a big success. The basic recipe is found in my favorite cookbook, *The Vegetarian Epicure*. By tripling the rum, cinnamon, and almond extract, using gingersnaps for the crust instead of graham crackers, and using Callebaut, the best Belgian chocolate that money can buy, it became an original. I have not found another cheesecake like it, and I have never heard a complaint!

JEWISH LESBIAN SUPPORT GROUP AND SEDERS

Marilyn Mesh and Barbara Esrig

In 1981, a group of us in Gainesville, FL, decided to start what became our Jewish lesbian consciousness-raising (CR) group. We called all the Jewish lesbians we knew. Admittedly, there were not a lot at first. At the first meeting it was Barbara Esrig, Marilyn Mesh, Ruth Segal, Lee and Diane Rogers (sisters), and Randi Cameon, and it was held at Marilyn's house.

Barbara Esrig: We all had had the experience that although as a lesbian community we were exploring our own internalized racism, ageism, and lookism, whenever we brought up anti-Semitism in the lesbian community, there was an uncomfortable pause and womyn would continue without acknowledgment. So the idea was to get together as a support group and to find a place together to explore who we were as Jews, examining our personal history and how we were evolving into our new lesbian-feminist context.

I remember that when we first started to meet together, some womyn who were not Jewish really did not understand the importance of us forming this affinity group and accused us of being exclusive. They even said it was a form of privilege for us to form this kind of group. This actually reinforced our need to meet together to explore and examine these accusations and not feel isolated in what we perceived as anti-Semitic remarks.

Marilyn Mesh: The thing I remember is immediately feeling so comfortable with the womyn there. No one said that my exuberance was "too much." That was OK with everyone. We were all ignited. We talked about certain struggles we had with some of our non-Jewish friends and lovers about this "exuberance" we had.

Culturally, as Jewish womyn and certainly as Jewish lesbians, we are neither quiet nor retiring. We are not pushed by what is proper, but rather by what our passion is. So this CR group had little to do with our religious affiliation of being Jewish. We were much more interested in our cultural similarities.

Barbara: And how we were in the world. After that first meeting, we were so excited we decided to get together once a month, and each CR meeting would have a topic that affected us differently because of having been raised Jewish, topics such as our relationship to self-expression, the role of social activism, our relationship to our family, our relationship to money, even to our sexuality. It was so revealing and exciting, and we learned so much about ourselves through these discussions.

Marilyn: Many lesbians had disassociated from their family at that time, but for many of us, the idea of completely cutting off our family just didn't feel right. We often found ourselves talking at the same time excitedly, and no one told the other to be quiet or to stop interrupting!

Barbara: It is not uncommon at, say, a Jewish family dinner table, to see and hear everyone talking at once, over each other. Many of us had had the experience of our non-Jewish friends and partners viewing this as (what they saw as) rude, pushy, or interrupting, while we saw it as interested and enthusiastic!

Marilyn: There was a feeling of safety here . . . Oh my God, I just kept thinking that here I can be all that I am. I did not feel any part of me was being pressed down, pushed in, tied up. I could be effusive, as loud as I wanted. Feeling safe was really important.

Barbara: When Passover came, we all decided to have a Jewish lesbian Seder. We also decided that this was a family ritual, and we wanted our non-Jewish partners and roommates to come if they sincerely wanted to come. At the time, Marilyn was living with Beckie Dale and Lynda Lou Simmons, so they went to the first one. Randi was with Corky, so Corky was there, too. Although both of their living arrangements have long since changed and changed again, Lynda Lou, Beckie and Corky have come to almost every Seder since then.

We never saw the Seder as just another party. It was an important Jewish ritual, part of our childhood, some part of that cultural heritage that we wanted to preserve. But as important as that ritual was and is to us, we also were well aware that there were parts of it that we could no longer conform to, so, as we do as lesbian-feminists, we rewrote it, transformed it, to make it ours.

Marilyn: At first we used the P'nai Or/Jewish Renewal Haggadah, which was very progressive but not lesbian specific. Then I got Judith Stein's lesbian Haggadah, and that's what we used until I made our own Haggadah sometime in the '80s. I've revised it several times since then. It grows as we do.

Haggadah cover with art by Judith Masur, whose Big Woman notecards are popular for feminist Haggadahs. (See www.judithmasurfinearts.com.)

Barbara: We no longer do our CR group. Those days are gone. But thirty-eight years later, the commitment to our Lesbian-Feminist Seder has remained strong—even stronger because new womyn have come and joined us, and every year they come because it is very important to all of us. For years now we have been twenty-five strong, and we all come back most every year. As the years have progressed, we have outgrown having the Seder at one of our houses, and now we do it in a large room at the Gainesville Pride Center.

Marilyn: As we grow older it is important to remember those feelings, memories connecting us to the past (and hopefully connecting us to the future) to recognize this one day of the year. Every year—for over thirty-five years—we do the same ritual, our ritual, and knew, and remembered. It's important.

JEWDYKE IN SHICKSAVILLE

Merril Mushroom

I grew up in Miami Beach, FL, during World War II. Even though the area originally was settled by rich gentiles from the North who wanted a place that was Jew-free, by the end of the war, in spite of the many "restricted" (no Jews allowed) areas, the population was mostly Jewish. My family was observant but not orthodox, and we engaged in Jewish customs, ceremonies, and rituals.

In Florida, most of my friends were gay/lesbian and Jewish, and after I moved to New York City in the 1960s, so were my friends there. As I became more feminist in my perspective, I rejected the patriarchal Jewishness that I was finding to be so oppressive. But as time went by, I realized that I missed the customs, ceremonies, and observances. I began to try to figure out ways to feminize the way I embraced my Jewishness.

Lo and behold, I found that other lesbian-feminist Jews were doing the same.

In 1980, I started attending Womonwrites—the annual Southeast Lesbian Writers' Conference. In 1997, we all decided that meeting once a year in the spring was not enough for our lesbian souls, and we began to meet again in the fall as well. When one of those fall gatherings was scheduled during the weekend of Yom Kippur by that year's gentile planners, we few Jewish Womonwriters were unhappy and disappointed. We often had experienced this sort of "oversight" in our everyday heteropatriarchal world of Christians, who frequently scheduled meetings and events meant for everyone during the High Holy Days, but we had hoped for better from our lesbian-feminist sisters, especially since these holidays were hardly kept secret from the general public. But the Womonwrites camp reservations had been made and could not be changed. We Jewesses discussed various ways we could deal with this: perhaps making a fuss, maybe girlcotting the conference. In the end, we realized that there were, in fact, no folks with whom we would rather spend time during this most important of Jewish holidays than our Womonwrites sisters.

So we made this into a learning experience for everyone who cared to participate. We led a workshop on the High Holy Days, explained about the Days of Awe, and talked about our lesbian femininization of the rituals. We had a Q&A for the shicksas. We held two events during which we combined Rosh Hashana and Yom Kippur rituals—one for Jewdykes only, and one for everyone who wished to attend. Our lesbian-feminized ritual began with a circle during which we called in our ancestors as well as living women who were not with us in the flesh. We did tashlich at the lake, casting off both personal and societal transgressions. We transformed that which we had cast off into what we wanted to bring to the coming year. We spoke of atonement in terms of at-one-ment. In place of the blowing of the shofar we did a group toning. Altogether, it was lovely.

We also did Shabbats at Womonwrites. Because the few of us Jewesses all were Caucasian and looked like all the white Christians, we felt a need to be ethnically visible. So on Shabbat we set up a table at lunchtime in the dining hall and did ritual with candles, wine, and challah. We sang shabbat songs and reminisced in our loud Jewish voices. We shared what we had done with our families and our Jewish lesbian communities back home—if we had them. We discussed any problems we saw on the horizon. The table was restricted to Jews only, while lovers and allies set up their own table nearby. But the dining hall was too noisy for intense, personal conversation, so after a few years, we retired our Oneg Shabbat to the porch where we could have more personal, intimate, Jewish conversations. And Alison, our gentile cook for several years, took it upon herself to include in the camp food order a challah for our shabbat table—a rare act of acknowledgment that warmed our hearts.

Outside of Womonwrites, in my everyday life, I observed the holidays that were significant to me in my own dykely way, sometimes alone, sometimes with others. Beside the High Holy Days, the most significant ritual of my childhood was Passover and the seders with my extended family. Grandma would do the customary two seders, each for upward of thirty people, and Grandpa would read the Haggadah and conduct the prayers while we kids would sneak swallows of wine and steal the afikomen. So I found a great deal of comfort in the many and varied lesbian and other woman-inclusive seders that were happening throughout the lesbian communities here in the South wherever there were Jewish dykes.

Basically, we observed Passover as a time of exodus, of hope, of freedom from slavery, freedom from whatever we felt bound by, freedom to move toward a better time. Our ritual objects on the seder plate had feminist significance—a raw egg for fertility of mind and spirit, a chicken bone for all the work we were expected to do because we were women and from which we could free ourselves, an olive to represent the Arab people who were suffering under the occupation by Israel, an orange because those who opposed women as rabbis would cite the incongruity by saying that having a woman rabbi is like having an orange on the seder plate—totally inappropriate. We had *moror* for the bitterness of oppression, greens for the promise of springtime and the renewal of the earth, and *charoses* for mortar to signify that women can build anything, especially out of food. We read from many different counterculture *haggadot*.

On Succot we built a Sukkah out of wood from the land we lived on—bamboo and cedar branches. We praised the harvest, and we thanked Mother Earth for all she gives to us, blessed her, and promised to care for her and to urge others to do the same.

On Purim we would have lesbian/gay/hippie costume parties. We would serve *hamantashen*, which were supposed to represent

Haman's three-cornered hat, but I always thought they looked more like cunts. We would read Judith Stein's *megillah*, which was a conversation between Esther, Zeresh, and Vashti. We made sure to emphasize the fact that Esther may have saved the Jews, but the real shero of the story was Vashti, because she was banished for standing up to the man and refusing to be sexually exploited when her husband the king demanded that she dance naked for his generals and royal buddies. After she was banished from the court, Esther, who was more compliant, was given to the king by her cousin Mordechai.

I never did like the heteropatriarchal war story of Chanukah, so when I became re-observant, I made it a holiday emphasizing miracles, which, to me, is the most significant part of the story of Chanukah. I lit each of the candles in the menorah for a miracle in my life, which was everything important and wonderful.

Now I live in a very small, very rural, very Christian county in Tennessee. There is a handful of Jews here, all lesbian, gay, queer, and an old hippie or two. I am cautiously open about being a Jew, but most of the local folks never have considered that anyone could possibly not be a Christian. Prayer is taken for granted as a part of life—Christian prayer, of course (as if there were any other kind). Prayers to Jesus often are recited before public gatherings, "blessings" said before meals, ball games, and other events and gatherings. It has been like this for the forty-five years I have lived here, and I take it as a part of the culture here and tolerate it, although I do not bow my head, close my eyes, or murmur amen, and I certainly am not doing anything in Jesus's name. So imagine my surprise when at a luncheon meeting with a local women's group, the hostess asked if I'd like to do a Jewish blessing before the meal. I said I would love to—do a Jewish-pagan prayer. I proceeded to say the *hamotzi* in Hebrew, then English, and thanked Mother Earth for providing us with sustenance and vowed to treat her with respect, kindness, and gratitude. No "in Jesus's name," but the women all "amen-ed" anyhow.

ALFA, AA, AND THE SPIRITUAL PATH
Lorraine Fontana

Because of the higher-than-average rate of alcoholism in the queer community, 12-Step groups grew in popularity and usefulness from the 1970s on. For the Atlanta Lesbian Feminist Alliance (ALFA), years of ongoing 12-Step meetings led to Dykes Together, an AA group for lesbians only that formed in 1977. Many of those who follow the 12-Step program see it as their spiritual journey and practice. Films like *Gay, Proud and Sober* (Image Associates, 21 minutes) led to discussions on spiritual development at such events as the September 1980 Southeast Lesbian Network meeting, and in 1982 there was a new anthology, *Out from Under: Sober Dykes and Their Friends*. In 1983 ALFA offered a series of programs on "the addiction crisis in the Atlanta lesbian and gay community" and efforts to make treatment programs more queer-friendly. This 12-Step thread had been around, and continued for years afterward as many lesbians found both community and relief from addiction through a spiritual path.

For some, sobriety and activism were incompatible, as in the story of an ALFA member who wrote "Why Recovering Women Leave the ALFA Community" (*Atalanta*, July 1987). She describes the basic fundamentals of the AA understanding of alcoholism and the spiritual nature of recovery for those 25% who maintain sobriety—the "reliance on a power greater than ourselves." She explains that since there are only three prognoses for alcoholism (insanity, death, or recovery), some who choose recovery hold on to that, literally, for dear life. Her "deep and effective spiritual experience" happened at a LEAP (Lesbians for Empowerment in Action & Politics) planner gathering in Gainesville, FL, where sober lesbians shared their stories.[1] Through these sisters, the "Goddess"

---

1 On LEAP, see *Sinister Wisdom* 93 (2014): 19 and *Sinister Wisdom* 109 (2018): 24–28.

became the higher power she could rely on, and other sober people became her family. Christina I. had a similar experience, writing *Atalanta* that she had to leave ALFA in order to maintain her sobriety:

> My thinking has to turn 180 degrees from negative to positive to recover from alcoholism. I must think and talk about the good in the world, not the bad. I must think and talk peace, and leave go of thinking or talking about war, or struggle, or oppression, or hatred. I must replace fear with faith in Life's need to express itself through me. This does not mean I have to turn into a saint, it simply means my thinking needs to stay on positive, spiritual principles. My soul must be in struggle with no one. To hate anyone, including male oppressors, even with justification, I have to hate myself, and internalization of self hate makes me uncomfortable enough to drink. You can see how these attitudes are much different than my radical lesbian political thinking.[2]

The AA stories that follow show how, on the contrary, others came to a 12-Step spiritual path through lesbian-feminist activism and community.

---

2 *Atalanta* 14.7 (1987): 3.

CONSTANT CRAVING: SEX, SAFETY, AND SOBRIETY

Sus Austill

Waves of adrenaline rushing with the incoming tide, I quickly strip off my clothes and run into the cold waters off Jacksonville Beach in Florida as midnight ushers in my twenty-first birthday. Too much alcohol to feel fear. The dark pier casting sharp moon shadows on wet sand.

Later that day, Roverta "Bo" Boen, owner of the Crowbar, a beach bar on North 1st Street, sends word to be at the bar that night if interested in working for her. We sit celebrating, well away from the double doors as firecrackers, smoke bombs, and other projectiles sometimes make it past the barrier built to protect patrons and employees. I felt honored, as Bo was a legend in her own time, known throughout the Southeast for opening the first gay bar in 1964 on Phillips Highway in Jacksonville. An older butch woman drinking a few feet away raises her beer mug to acknowledge our celebration. An hour later she is brutally attacked with baseball bats while walking on the same sand I stood shivering on the night before. Sirens piercing through a familiar tune from the jukebox blend with images of a mangled face. This was my rite of passage into dyke adulthood as I immersed in alcohol and secrecy for emotional survival.

This was the late seventies in Florida. Anita Bryant had dealt a heavy blow to the hopes of the gay community.[1] The AIDS epidemic was not yet identified. The lesbian community I had been part of in Miami smoked pot heavily; the bisexual community often dabbled in drugs and alcohol; the gay men used poppers, alcohol,

---

[1] See Merril Mushroom, "Anita Bryant, Florida, 1978," *Sinister Wisdom* 109 (2018): 14–16.

and heavier drugs. Across the gay community hung a curtain of defiance bolstered with addictive behaviors. Alcohol was often the first substance used to drown out messages of doubt, insecurity, or self-hatred as our families ostracized us or strangers called us an abomination in the name of God. So, we flocked to the bars or parties, eager to mingle, dance, and flirt, ignoring the ever-present potential of getting physically hurt on the way to or from a gay event.

Women were starting to gather in communities, both in rural and urban areas. The Lesbian Task Force in Miami began as part of NOW,[2] developed a life of its own, and nourished the souls of over one hundred lesbians in Miami. Many a day and night were spent at the home of Louise and Maryanne healing wounds inflicted by patriarchy. Running hard from the abuses inflicted by mostly men but also women in my teenage years, I found refuge. I grew in strength: learning tai chi, bicycling everywhere, working hard as the first female construction worker for the City of Miami Parks and Recreation Department. Alcohol flowed, and freshly rolled joints were passed from the very first night I joined the group.

Young lesbians struggled to define themselves in new ways. They were neither butch nor femme. They weren't quite granola lesbians either. The increase of women in the workforce meant we also developed some of the diseases more identified with men. Women dying of heart attacks and cirrhosis increased. Lesbians were suffering from alcoholism at rates as high as 54%, compared to 10% of the straight population and as high as 81% among gay men.

Sickness, suicides, and violence directed toward us as individuals and our communities escalated our isolation, addictive behaviors, and fear of anyone reaching out with the hand of God to help. Yet as the 1980s began, so did the emergence of detox centers, followed by treatment centers. New research—the Godwin

---
2 National Organization for Women

studies, indicating a genetic proponent to the development of alcoholism—left jails and hospitals open to liability lawsuits if they refused to treat alcoholics. These new programs found a ready-made resource, the Twelve Steps of recovery practiced in Alcoholics Anonymous (AA).

However, these same steps served as a barrier for most in the gay community. For example, the Third Step of AA was terrifying:

"Turn your will and life over to God, as you understand him."

What did that really mean? Were we to be judged as abominations? Did sobriety mean becoming straight? For those who had already come to terms with themselves through MCC[3] or finding acceptance with the Goddess came the next challenges, Steps Four and Five.

Step Four: "Complete a searching and fearless moral inventory of ourselves."

Abomination loomed even larger in this step. We told lies, denied reality, and omitted truths to not lose family, friends, and employment. Subterfuge was normal for us; it was an act of survival. Not able to marry our partners, we marked "single" on applications. Partners maintained separate bedrooms and were introduced as "friends." We attended special events with a "beard"[4] or didn't attend at all. Lesbian sex was disregarded as "not real sex" or pathologized;[5] so we didn't discuss our sex life with our health care providers, and they didn't ask.

Step Five: "Admit to God, to ourselves, and to another human being the exact nature of our wrongs."

---

3 Metropolitan Community Church

4 A man willing to impersonate a love interest to avoid questions at office parties, etc. Women who did this for gay men were known as "skirts."

5 Prior to 2012, Centers for Disease Control did not recognize lesbians as having sex, and though data on female-to-female transmission was being submitted, they discarded the data.

This was a challenging task for gay people joining groups of AA members raised in the Bible Belt. I remember sitting in a room full of people urging me to let go of the shame of alcoholism while ignoring the internalized sexual shaming caused by religion. The unspoken AA attitude in north Florida at the time toward a gay person was "hate the sin, love the sinner," with expectations that the newly recovering person would change their ways when they sobered up.

Desperate for sobriety in 1981 as my life was falling apart and homophobes cheered as gay men were dying en masse of the "gay curse," I concluded that recovery meant becoming "straight." After all, this new way of life demanded I go to any length for a new way of life.

I changed jobs, moved, married a person of opposite gender, and birthed a child, all in my first year without alcohol, despite an unspoken rule in AA to *not* make any major life changes during that time. The marriage ended prior to my child's second birthday. I played Cris Williamson tapes to bring back times of being among lesbians in Miami, dancing bare-breasted on full moons at the Veteran's Counseling Center, munching on raw veggies, and, most of all, feeling powerful.

Turning thirty years old in 1987 brought a woman into my life who rocked my world. Sober, intelligent, spiritual, and a lesbian . . . she touched my heart. She worked the twelve steps of AA and knew of healing beyond AA doctrine. She sparked my truth. I love women. We talked, cried, and shared. My second child, in utero, would soon make her presence known, leading to our breakup at three months of gestation. Newborns were not present in the lesbian community of the South yet.

The pregnancy brought a renewed interest in going to any length for my sobriety. A single mom of two, I found a lesbian therapist, reached out to lesbian coworkers, and began attending the Calendar of Events (COE) Lesbian Potlucks in nearby Jacksonville. My breastfeeding a six-day-old newborn did receive mixed reactions from lesbians there, but no one said I did not belong or needed to change. I found lesbians who were kid-friendly and supportive of recovery. Linda Thornton of Gainesville organized a lesbian support group for the purpose of socializing and recreation. Her events were not based on alcohol consumption; when present, it was minimal.

Eventually, Emanon,[6] a gay and lesbian AA group, ironically began meeting in the basement of a Catholic church situated in downtown Jacksonville, a place of refuge surrounded by the political and financial reaches of the First Baptist Church. Their religious flock numbering in the thousands was known for leaving Sodom and Gomorrah pamphlets in bathrooms while their preacher, Homer Lindsay, Jr., blamed the AIDS epidemic on sinful behavior. The gay community poured most of its resources into caring for gay men fighting for their lives. This left fewer resources for lesbians who were winning custody of their children and, with the help of turkey basters, creating new families. Lesbians seeking sobriety found each other at AA meetings for women. The nurture, emotional availability, and much needed babysitting met the needs of myself and other young mothers as well as grandmothers. Women in AA understood the wounds of patriarchy as well as we did and welcomed us with open arms. Secrets were no longer needed for survival, and fantasy replaced hope. My rite of passage into adulthood was completed.

---

6 "No name" spelled backwards.

GETTING SOBER IN AA

Helen Renée Brawner

I began drinking in 1967, aged sixteen, and by 1969 was being told by the medical profession that I could not drink. I was not ready to stop and resented being told I could not continue. I slowed little, attempted controlled drinking, failed at each attempt, and continued contrary to health advice.

In 1971, after leaving a short-lived, hellish marriage, I dried out using Kundalini yoga. Then I moved to Tampa, FL, and began a descent into a new level of willingness to do whatever it took to be finished drinking. Tampa was rough, challenging, and there were alcohol and drugs at every turn. I lasted from May to October there and was ready to be anywhere the leaves were turning colors because of the colder temps, not merely from dehydration, and to live with my first lesbian partner.

In western North Carolina, living with a woman, I was drinking less, but drinking was a problematic part of our lifestyle. For six years our lives revolved around each other. We were isolated from other lesbians, unaware of the culture that was growing by leaps and bounds—even all over the South, including Asheville, which at that time was about an hour's drive away. My partner became ill, and our relationship dissolved without closure as she returned to Florida for medical treatment.

Left alone and isolated in 1978, my drinking was heavier than ever. Living in a dry county, and rarely able to get to a liquor store, I kept a supply of bottles and a gallon of white liquor on hand at all times. When I met the woman who would become a roommate for several years in a home nearer the college, she was appalled at the amount of liquor I consumed each evening after work. In 1979 she introduced me to the lesbian community in Asheville, including the woman who would eventually lead me to the open doors of Alcoholics Anonymous.

Spring of 1982, I had vowed to stop drinking and also to help a new partner to stop. Nobody ever suggested any program of recovery or rehabilitation despite numerous alcohol-related problems and bouts of depression. I wondered how a lesbian in the Asheville community had stopped and seemed happier and less angry than she had while drinking. One evening I went to a *Womyn Together* newsletter meeting in Asheville and knew I would drink if I started home without something or someone intervening. I decided to take a chance and go to that sober woman's home and ask her what she had done to get sober.

She was already dressed for bed and answered the door in a long chenille bathrobe. When she heard why I was on her stoop, she welcomed me inside and to her sofa, explaining that she had gone to a meeting at Michigan Womyn's Music Festival. There she was encouraged to go back home and attend AA meetings there, even if there were few women. One of the performers at MWMF had shared that while attending a meeting back home the speaker, a man with whom she thought she had nothing in common, had told her story! She had returned to Asheville and begun attending both women's and mixed AA meetings.

I attended a noon meeting the next day. I learned there had been an attempt to have a lesbian meeting earlier, but none of the women had enough time to keep it going or support one another at that time. I was able to help other women by managing a women's halfway house, taking women to meetings, and showing others that a lesbian can live happily without alcohol.

Angry at religion and the God of my childhood, my first higher power was a corporation who sent someone to start my car and make my days more manageable—a true test of whether the relationship was working. I resented the references to God in the literature but soon was able to hear that even the atheists were welcome and found a way to stay sober in AA. My anger softened, and my love of nature, which had seen me through many hard times in childhood and early adulthood, returned. I embraced the goddess and found my own way of connecting with deity and the ancestors.

It would be 1989 before another lesbian started a lesbian and gay AA meeting in Asheville. Meanwhile, many lesbians have found a way to get sober and stay sober through AA. Each of us has found her own spiritual connection, referred to in recovery circles as a "higher power," often beginning as a group of caring individuals but evolving into a relationship with the inner self, a deity, or a way of being that is conducive to sobriety and the pursuit of serenity.

I GET DRY WITH A LITTLE HELP FROM MY FRIENDS

Kathleen "Corky" Culver,
from an interview with Barbara Esrig[1]

Part of my motivation for getting sober was that I had just seen an antinuclear protest ending with the arrests of activists. I wanted to be willing to go to jail for justice but thought I would have a hard time not being able to drink in jail. I knew that to be free enough to act on my beliefs, I had to give up drinking.

We were part of an antinuclear group organizing against the proliferation of nuclear submarine stations, power plants, and weapons. We listened to Helen Caldicott. We demanded the cleanup of radioactive waste dump sites and the closure of nuclear reactors until they dealt with important repairs and critical safety issues. Our group had just been asked to join a large demonstration at the Savannah River Nuclear Power Plant in South Carolina, where we would block the entrance so workers couldn't go in.

I and five lesbian friends—Kate Gallagher, Lynda Lou Simmons, Judy Keathley, Pam Smith, and Jean Francis from the Gainesville group—decided we would be ready to risk going to jail for civil disobedience. I quit drinking for three days before we set off for the Peace Camp where the demonstration was being coordinated.

We all camped out together, and I remember we made a circle to introduce ourselves and so we could each speak our truth. It was very orderly, and everyone listened when another person spoke without interruptions or cross talk. That was normal protocol in

---

[1] Barbara Esrig interviewed Corky Culver in Melrose, FL, November 21, 2019. This interview was not recorded, but the complete 1593-word interview notes are archived. Culver has also written about the action in South Carolina and the Peacewalk to Key West described here in "Into the Grueling Duelings of Consensus Dances Sweet Meditation," *Sinister Wisdom* 93 (2014): 23–26.

group process at the time. There was no shell or talking stick back then, so instead we passed around a fifth of Southern Comfort. When it was my turn and I was handed the bottle, I passed it to the next woman without taking a drink.

I remember feeling nervous and self-conscious because everybody in the circle knew that I wanted to stop drinking. I didn't know how they would react. Much to my surprise, after me, a couple more women passed the bottle without taking a sip either! I was so surprised when they did that. It really felt like I was getting unexpected support.

After a few days of planning meetings, we mobilized for the blockade. It wasn't just us but a huge group of men and women. All of us had talked about the dangers of nuclear power with the local people who lived around the Savannah plant and were getting cancer. Then my friends and I joined others, took a stand by the plant entrance, locked arms, and refused to leave. We allowed ourselves to be forcibly removed and arrested and would not give our names. Each called herself "Jane Doe," knowing that would get us in jail. (Actually, the policeman who arrested me put my stated name down as "John Doe," a dig at my dyke look.) Sure enough, the six of us were carted off to the Bamberg County Detention Center.

Getting handcuffed, put in a van, and taken to an unknown place was scary, but lo and behold, they put the Gainesville group in the same cell block! The block consisted of pairs of cells with only bars between them, and in the very next cell was Blue Lunden. Blue was one of the women who lived at Sugarloaf Women's Community, a center for nonviolence on Sugarloaf Key, FL, with Barbara Deming, a well known peace activist. Because she was a recovered alcoholic herself, Blue's wise, knowledgeable, and kind way helped me in those crucial days of early sobriety, as well as the fact that no alcohol was available.

The idea of being in jail was terrifying, but once there we actually felt powerful, and lucky. We were in jail for sixteen days.

I think the sheriff really sympathized with our protest, and he helped make our time there not easy, but bearable. We even had a jail block Halloween party with makeshift costumes. The sheriff left our cell doors open so we could move around the block and visit each other. Barbara Deming sent us cookies.

We were interviewed by several newspapers and referenced in national news on NPR. The press gave us access to the outside, and a lot of people knew where we were. For all those reasons we never felt isolated or alone.

In jail we had difficult discussions about when we would give our names to start the sentencing and release process. Some did not want to give our names until there were no more missiles, some when there were no more wars, and some wanted desperately to get back to their lives. We were stuck, and the arguments continued.

At that point we decided to meditate together. We put down a green blanket, pretended it was grass (ha!), and sat in a circle. We asked for guidance deep within, and that is how the Peace Walk was envisioned. Out of the meditation came the image and idea of all of us as a sort of cleansing, flowing stream. We saw a peaceful demonstration, walking from Gainesville all the way to Key West. In meditation we saw we could get attention by walking through every little town along the route. It was a way to both continue our mission and get out of jail.

When released, we all wanted to eat really good food and celebrate together. At the restaurant, my friends surrounded me on one side of the table where no one drank. It was a crucial time for me. I had not known if I could have a good time, if I could socialize, without drinking. It was wonderful to feel the healing.

The subsequent support I got from my community was amazing. In part because of my choice to give up alcohol, it was decided the Peace Walk would be chem-free, clean and sober. That was a wonderful way for us to be together. A group connected by optimism and idealism is a beautiful thing.

On the Peace Walk, which lasted forty days, we sang and chanted all the way down the Florida peninsula. It was high-minded. The local television, radio, and newspapers helped to spread the word about our action and broaden support. Every night people offered places where we could stay. One night we slept inside a Mexican restaurant! We had circles every day to discuss our mission, our worries, our blisters, and plans. We had the precious experience of living together, sharing a life-changing experience, and getting stronger.

Photo by Emily Greene

Peacewalk begins downtown Gainesville, December 17, 1983. Corky Culver is holding the sign at left, Blue Lunden at right. Peacewalkers carried the sign all the way to Key West on a forty-one-day walk.

Along the route, we met many lesbians and began introducing them to our experience with activism as a way to engage rather than drinking. During that time in the 1980s, some lesbians thought that the only way to meet other lesbians was by going to bars. Perhaps we helped sow the seeds of sobriety for some.

After the Peace Walk came more actions, conferences, and community building. We had consciousness-raising (CR) meetings where a subject was given, and everyone talked about how they related to that subject. When a CR was offered on addictions, I became uptight, fearing that the whole focus would be on me. Amazingly, it was not. Instead, there was not a single person out of thirty-four in the circle who didn't have a personal connection to addiction, either their own or a family member's.

Those of us who thought we were alone found out that many other people had what we thought was our own personal failing or drama. Suddenly, we were relieved from all that self-condemnation. The once–heavily drinking community now supported other activities, like chem-free dances. We discovered that we did not have to deal with problems alone.

We learned we could do it together.

MOBLEY-IZING FOR CHANGE: A BLACK LESBIAN SEEKING COMMUNITY IN THE SOUTH

Woody Blue from Lorraine Fontana's interview with Carolyn Mobley[1]

In the '70s, throughout the United States, lesbians were figuring it out. They may have started slow and tentative, but once out of the closet, lesbians formed their own societies and social clubs. There were sports clubs for the jocks, speakeasies for the discreet professionals, bars for meetups and dancing, bridge clubs, bowling leagues, groups that tangoed, and the Girl Scouts. LOL. There was lots of adventure to be had. Crushing out on gym teachers was big. Sleepovers and kissing girls. That kind of thing.

There was one woman, born in Sanford, FL (December 17, 1948), who never doubted that she belonged in the lesbian world. Her name is Carolyn Mobley. Her granddaddy was a Baptist preacher, and many generations of church blood trickled through her veins. Being in the church was in her DNA.

Carolyn was a member first and foremost of the Black community where she was raised and baptized at age ten. By the time she was through high school she was sure she was a lesbian. Being the adventurous type, she elected to attend a predominantly white coed college in Abilene, TX, thinking that would keep her lesbian tendencies at bay. Surprise! Despite constantly crushing out on (or finding herself attracted to) white girls, she managed to get her religious education degree in 1971.

In those days, women weren't allowed to become preachers. Carolyn wasn't into "bucking the system"; she just wanted to serve God and knew that was her vocation. And just because, she fell

---

[1] Lorraine Fontana interviewed Carolyn Mobley by phone on December 15, 2015.

in love with a European American, Southern Baptist missionary woman in the Bahamas. Hmm, well she could not let this interfere with her future; could she?

She hightailed it up to Orlando and started work at Shiloh Baptist Church as their youth director and minister of education. She was doing her dream, not preaching but working in a Black church, finding her way. That path included a couple of exciting lesbian affairs that she survived and that gave her some real-life experience.

In 1973, Carolyn headed toward Atlanta to attend seminary. Seminary offers a Master's degree that takes two to three years to complete, and is usually required to become an ordained preacher or hold higher positions in most churches. This level of schooling has been a stumbling block for many Blacks who have a calling. Some Black traditions did not require school, figuring God could select whomever God wanted, and one did not need formal education for ordination. But Carolyn had her sights set on creating inclusivity and diversity in the Christian Church and was willing to spend the time it took to reach ordination.

Atlanta is a big city, and Carolyn was ready to meet her challenges. She "grew up as a lesbian" during her days at seminary, exploring the gay lifestyle outside the classroom. Upon graduation in 1976, before she joined, she became involved, with the MCC denomination (a church ministering to a predominantly gay congregation) and got a paying job as a career missionary working for the conservative Southern Baptist Convention. It was kind of an oil and water mix.

Carolyn worked with the Southern Baptists for five years before they approached her about whether she was gay. She refused to lie to give an answer, and they told her she would have to answer or resign. She agreed to resign. She told them, "I'd rather leave than stay in a church that believes you either have to be [thought of as] a whore or a homosexual, nothing in between, if one is single."

You could kick Carolyn Mobley out of the Church, but you couldn't kick the Church out of Carolyn Mobley. She headed out the Baptist church door in 1981 and immediately became a formal member of the first MCC Church in Atlanta. Later that year she attended her first pride march. You can't keep a good woman down. She got a "no-brainer" job as a courier, working for Central Delivery through a former Baptist professor friend who had also been thrown out of his job at a Baptist university. Over the next several years, she worked her way through the ranks—driver, foot carrier, then customer service rep, making more money than she was paid working for the church.

Enthusiastically she jumped into the gay and lesbian social activities that were blossoming in the Atlanta area. Carolyn had always loved to sing. She became a soloist with the Atlanta Feminist Women's Chorus and also sang with Lambda Choral, the coed gay and lesbian chorus. She went to every pride march, playing her guitar and singing community songs at LGBT rallies and gatherings.

In 1981 the ugly specter of AIDS reared its head. Carolyn met it head-on, getting trained as an AIDS educator. As a volunteer for the Gay Community Center, she advocated for people living with AIDS, and as a deacon for the MCC Church, she conducted funerals for those that died.

This was a time when gay women were redefining themselves; identifying as lesbian, separatist, and radical; and struggling to live in a patriarchal society that wanted to shut them out. Many women of color adopted a feminist perspective but found their doctrines lacking. An alternative analysis called "womanism" found ground in the South. As Alice Walker describes it, "Womanist is to feminist as purple is to lavender." Womanism was born primarily from the Black women theologians who were infiltrating the Christian seminaries. They contended that the African American woman's experience could not be described by Black male theologians or white feminists.

Carolyn Mobley struggled to define her own place between these two paradigms. She found community in the LGBT social groups (she now thinks of them as too Eurocentric), which catered to a mostly white population. She visited ALFA house to experience a feminist environment and to learn more (see ALFA story, this issue), but there were few women of color. She also leaned toward a womanist perspective, which felt true to her Black experience. However, that perspective also included men, and Carolyn, as a lesbian, liked the idea of women's space without men. As a Black lesbian, she couldn't separate the two identities in herself. In the end she embraced both philosophies, blending them in ways that made sense to her as she struggled to advance in the Church and participate in her social circles.

This was a common struggle for Black gays in the white-dominated movement, particularly in the South, where civil rights issues had come to a head in recent history. Though proclaiming inclusive values, the LGBT community's deeply entrenched racist upbringing still dictated newly formed policies. Carolyn describes a time in Atlanta when gay bars were double IDing Black men in an effort to keep them out. Black issues were often pushed to the side when white lesbians organized events. Carolyn understood that racism underlay the LGBT movement, but instead of turning away, she worked within to make concrete change. This was the belief that steered her in all her communities and clarified the struggle as a female preacher in the Southern Christian churches, as a Black lesbian in a white gay community, and as a lesbian in the Black community.

In efforts to connect the gay community with the Black community, Carolyn helped start a group called the African American Lesbian Gay Alliance with Marque Walker, a well known gay activist from Morehouse College. This group celebrated Blacks of all spiritual backgrounds, including those outside Christianity, providing faith-based services. Carolyn stayed active in this group while she lived in Atlanta.

Toward the late '80s, she quit her job as a courier and worked for a time at Charis, a feminist bookstore, entertaining the idea of eventually becoming one of four part-owners. That did not materialize, and Carolyn yearned for a life where she could use her education and experience.

The pull of the Church was strong. In 1990, she accepted a position with the Resurrection MCC Church in Houston, TX, bringing all her skills, life experience, and enthusiasm with her. She was welcomed with open arms and after only two years was elected to be the Grand Marshal in the Houston Pride Parade.

For the next fifteen years she worked in the MCC Church as a leader. She continued to assist in the AIDS-torn community and provided a listening ear to those seeking help. Her singing in the choir was inspirational; her exuberance was contagious. She became one of the longest-serving MCC clergy at Resurrection. She was the first and only Black woman when she started; when she left, there were paid African Americans on staff, and *more* African Americans were in the congregation. When she left, her congregation honored her by hosting a casino-styled party, advertised as "Holy Craps"; her parting gift to the community was a "Sing the Love" concert, in which she was featured along with the Gospel Ensemble she helped to start years before.

The Black lesbian experience in the South, as well as the rest of the country, is far different from that of white women. Black lesbians' push to have an equal footing in the larger society has not been well documented, and the tragedies, disappointments, and internal conflicts of individuals are still buried and hidden from public viewing.

Throughout her life, Carolyn has struggled to incorporate her visions into society to create a better world. From a young age she realized she wanted to work in the Church to serve God. Putting the dream into action required a strong backbone. Living in the South, in an environment that was hesitantly moving forward to integrate its Black and white populations, meant that Carolyn needed to call into play all her people skills. She has been a mediator, a spiritual leader, and a role model for those who share her vision.

In Houston, she was interviewed as the 1992 Grand Marshal for the pride parade. She was asked, "Who are your people?"

Carolyn Mobley (right) and her partner, Adrain Barre.

Well, actually all people. But I have three groups that I identify primarily with as my people. First of all, Black people are my people. You know, that's how I grew up. That was the first way I understood myself in the world, was as a Black person so Black folk are my people. And I said, gay folk are my people. All gay, lesbian, bisexual, transgender people are my people because I also identify as lesbian. And I said, church people are my people. I love the folk outside the church too, but I've chosen to train and live and work through the church. And so, those are my people. Black folk, gay folk, and Christian folk. Even the bad ones among them. I know Christianity has some serious problems—with the right-wing side—but there's enough pull the left side to bring us closer to the center, and that's where I am in MCC.

MCC is where I am theologically about inclusion too. I stay with MCC because I believe in the dream. The dream is a place that is multicultural, multiracial, everybody on the same level playing field. Nobody is there yet, but we're moving in that direction. We have from day one—that's been the intention; that's been the goal.

Carolyn Mobley currently lives in Saginaw, MI, with her partner of almost twenty years, whom she legally married on her birthday, December 17, 2016, while living in and serving a church in Richmond, VA. She continues to sing, preach, and extol the Lord in her attempts to move heaven and earth.

FELICIA AND BARB AND BORK: LESBIAN-FEMINIST ACTIVISM IN ALABAMA

Merril Mushroom, from an interview with
Felicia Fontaine and Barb Collins[1]

Felicia Fontaine and Barb Collins have been married three times—to each other. Huntsville, AL, residents since 1982, they have been involved in lesbian-feminist activism all their lives. This is their story:

Felicia was born in Johnson City, TN. Her first feminist activism was in 1971 when she was in high school. "We decided we were going to break the dress code. Girls were required to wear skirts, and it was cold, so we decided that on a certain day, we were going to wear pants." The entire senior class showed up in pants, and the dress code was changed system-wide. Her grandfather was pastor of a large independent Christian church, and her life was immersed in the church. She always was a tomboy. "I had always known I wasn't a girly girl. I didn't want to be anyone's damn princess."

Barb was born in Hampton, VA, where her father was in the army. After he got out, the family moved to a German Catholic town in Missouri, where they lived in a tavern. During her childhood, Barb "had every kind of doll, a whole kitchen set-up.... All the girls from the neighborhood would come over and play with it. I'd go out and play war with their brothers."

In school, they both had crushes on the cheerleaders, not the football players.

In 1966, Barb joined the navy, and in 1969 she left the navy, got married, had a baby, got a divorce, and came out of the closet. In 1974, she says, "They changed the laws so you could have a child

---

[1] Rose Norman interviewed Felicia Fontaine and Barb Collins at their Huntsville home on November 14, 2013.

and serve, so I went back in the navy." However, they had not yet changed the laws to enable openly gay persons to serve.

Felicia studied counseling in college and felt called to go into the ministry. Her goal was to be a prison chaplain. While she was in college, her own therapist helped her to reconcile that she could be a Christian and be gay. She graduated, broke up with her first lover, moved to Memphis, and met Barb. Although Barb didn't know it at the time, her own first lover Jeannie was breaking up with her. The navy had sent Barb to Norfolk, and she left her daughter with Jeannie in the house they had together. She found out about the breakup over the telephone.

Everyone except Barb knew that Jeannie intended to break up with her when she returned, and Felicia, who had been interested in Barb since they'd first met, "decided I was deliberately going to go courting." She did, and they did, and eventually they moved to Alabama together with Barb's daughter Carol.

Conditions for lesbians and gay men in the navy had gotten much worse after Reagan became president. Before that, the emphasis was on trying to catch gays in the service in the boot camps and Navy A Schools (first level of training for a specific rate or specialty). During the Reagan era, they focused more on trying to catch people who were getting close to retirement, to get rid of them before they had to be paid. Barb thought maybe she had better get out while she could because she had been way too open, and the Reagan folks had put out a memo that the prohibition against homosexuality applied to women—lesbians—as well as men. Felicia said, "When Reagan was elected, I saw less hope of us surviving as a couple in the navy."

But the resistance was beginning to rise. Frank Kameny, an astronomer with NASA, had been fired in 1959 for being homosexual. He sued the federal government and, after a ten-year lawsuit, won his case. As a result, President Gerald Ford signed an executive order protecting federal workers from gay discrimination firing. Now, gays and lesbians in the military were starting to come out and demand equal rights. Leonard Matlovich won his case before the Supreme Court for the air force to reinstate him after he was discharged dishonorably in 1975, but then he was denied entry to Langley AFB when he reported back to duty.

Mary Mitchell, who was stationed across the navy base from Barb, walked in and told her commander, "Not only yes, but hell yes, I am, so there!" When he refused to believe her, she publicly called herself "Mary Mitchell Queer." After she got out of the navy, she went to work for the federal government doing the same job she did in the navy for three times the pay. She could be out as a lesbian, and her job was protected thanks to the Kameny decision.

In 1980, Felicia and Barb were married through the MCC church. The term "holy union" had been used since 1973 because clergy in some states were being threatened over their performing "marriage" ceremonies. Barb's navy companions came to the wedding and were supportive and helpful.

Felicia, meanwhile, had completed her degree in computer science, and six months before Barb got out of the navy, they started looking for a place to relocate. They wanted to be south of the Mason-Dixon line and east of the Mississippi. They wouldn't consider Virginia or Florida because the social services folks were removing children from lesbian mothers. They were inclined toward Oak Ridge, TN, but job opportunities that worked out perfectly for them came along in Huntsville, and, according to Barb, "We decided God meant for us to be in Alabama."

In 1982, when Felicia was filling out the paperwork for her new job, she put down Barb and Carol on her health insurance. Her supervisor was taken aback. He had assumed that Felicia's roommate who was getting out of the navy was a man. Felicia told him they had been married in the Metropolitan Community Church and asked if he was questioning her religion. He put Barb and Carol on the policy with no more objections.

They became involved with Huntsville NOW, and in 1984 Felicia became president of the local chapter. Even before she took office, she was asked to intervene with "pro-life" picketers who had been harassing workers and patients at Alabama's women's clinics. Clinics were being vandalized, and women were being intimidated and even violently assaulted and attacked, all in the name of Christianity. The pro-choice women's community organized escort services to protect women entering the clinic. Felicia organized a counterdemonstration, and before she knew it, she had become the spokesperson for abortion rights.

Because of the strong anti-Christian reaction that resulted, Felicia was hesitant to be out about her calling to the ministry. "I really considered my activism an extension of my ministry. Jesus was a radical political activist, and we're called to follow in his footsteps." She did her feminist activism as a closeted Christian.

In 1984, they organized the Southeastern Conference for Lesbians and Gay Men in Birmingham. The Black mayor, Richard Arrington, Jr., came to the first plenary to welcome everyone and gave Meg Christian a key to the city.

After serving as president of Huntsville NOW, Felicia was elected president of the State of Alabama NOW. In early 1986, she and Barb got to see George Wallace sign a Women's History Month proclamation naming Rosa Parks and Angela Davis as great women from Alabama.

On July 1, 1987, President Ronald Reagan nominated Robert Bork to the U.S. Supreme Court, and Felicia began to organize to block his confirmation. Bork had followed Richard Nixon's orders to fire Special Prosecutor Archibald Cox during the Watergate Investigation. After Bork's appointment, Ted Kennedy delivered a "Robert Bork's America" speech before the Senate, which painted a dreadful picture of lost civil rights. Bork also was opposed to women's reproductive rights, including the right to birth control.

Alabama was important to the Bork nomination because Alabama's senior Senator Howell Heflin, a former chief justice of the Alabama Supreme Court, was a very influential member of the Senate Judiciary Committee. A coalition of folks from various justice organizations held a "Block Bork" rally in Birmingham after the first week of hearings in an attempt to encourage Heflin to listen to Bork more critically than he otherwise might. In the end, Heflin would not recommend Bork, and the Judiciary Committee voted 9–5 against recommending the appointment to the full senate. Bork asked for the Senate vote anyhow, and the Senate voted against his nomination 42–58. Felicia says, "It remains the most significant action with which I was associated."

After Bork's defeat, Anthony Kennedy filled that seat. Kennedy went on to write the four landmark decisions advancing LGBTQ rights, including the right to marry.

Felicia continued to work at the MCC church and the counseling center. She "brought that MCC kicking and screaming into social activism in 1989." She organized gay rights marches and protests against Cracker Barrel when that restaurant got national attention for homophobic behavior to servers. Felicia often would wear her clergy vestments to good advantage. When they applied for a permit to protest Cracker Barrel in Cullman, she dressed in full collar to attend the city council meeting that was also well attended by Klansmen. Barb says, "As soon as we got there, a Klan guy started writing down license numbers. So I got a piece of paper and started taking down license numbers." Felicia continues, "I wasn't aware of what a badass had turned up there until I turned the numbers over to Klanwatch."[2]

In 1992, the LGBT community wanted to hold their first open gay pride march, but they were denied a permit. So Felicia donned her vestments, went down to city hall, and asked for a permit. She says, "Whereas he [the clerk] had blown off this young gay man who had come in for the permit, he couldn't quite do that with me."

---

[2] Klanwatch was a watchdog of the Southern Poverty Law Center in Montgomery, AL. It is now run as a blog called Hatewatch that monitors the radical right. See splc.org.

In 1993, Felicia was diagnosed with multiple sclerosis. She retired from MCC in 1995 and continued her ministry through a private counseling practice and Soulforce Alabama. Through that, she led an effort to confront Alabama Chief Justice Roy Moore on dicta he issued analyzing Alabama law and homosexuality. At the time of their actual meeting, Felicia was in the middle of chemotherapy for breast cancer and was bald as an egg. He had committed to follow the ruling of the U.S. Supreme Court in the *Lawrence v. Texas* case that was pending at the time. For thirteen years, he kept his word until the issue of marriage equality arose.

Felicia (left) and Barb.

As for those three marriages, at the reception for the first one, in 1980, they had joked that if it worked out, in twenty years they would make it legal. In 2000, Vermont became the first state to offer legal recognition of single-sex couples. For their twentieth anniversary, almost to the minute, they were married by a JP in the town hall of Brattleboro, Vermont. After disposing of Roy Moore, they were married in Alabama on their thirty-fifth anniversary. The theme for the wedding: Third Time's the Charm.

PHYLLIS MEEK: PIONEER FOR GENDER NON-DISCRIMINATION POLICY

Phyllis Meek[1] interviewed by Barbara Esrig

What was the situation at the University of Florida (UF) between 1963 and 1966, you ask? I was hired on the dean of women's staff in 1966. There were very few women students because UF had been coed only about twenty years. Then in 1969 they created an Office for Student Development, and the two staffs merged. Of course, the dean of women didn't become the dean of students, the dean of men did. I became associate dean. I inherited supervising these men from the dean of men's staff, and they were not real happy with me. It worked out, though.

For example, they were used to their secretaries making coffee for them. When I became the associate dean, I'd go to the dean of men's office to make my own coffee. I was trying to set an example, and I started giving the men a lot of ribbing—the secretaries loved me for that. Some of the men left; some got more used to my being their supervisor. And they all started making their own coffee. Ironically, that was a hurdle for the women's movement in 1970. The secretaries were delighted because, you know, that was insulting to them.

UF Lesbian and Gay Students (UFLAGS) started in the early '80s. Before that there had been no mention of gay and lesbian people because of the attitude about the Johns Committee, and I think in general what society was like.[2] Previously, there really

---

1   Phyllis Meek died June 5, 2020.

2   Charley Johns, a Florida legislator (and acting governor 1953–55), led a McCarthy-like legislative committee that at first sought "communist fronts," and, not finding that, persecuted lesbians and gays, especially on university campuses. The actions of the Johns Committee forced the resignation of many faculty and administrators at UF, Florida State University, and the University of South Florida. The committee was active from 1956–65. See Merril Mushroom, "The Gay Kids and the Johns Committee," *Crooked Letter I*, ed. Connie Griffin (Montgomery, AL: NewSouth Books, 2015): 123–34.

was a purge. I mean, literally the Johns Committee went after any faculty who appeared to be gay, mainly men, because we didn't have that many women faculty, and some students as well. A lot of the men were forced to resign. It set up a terrible climate. Nothing changed until UFLAGS finally formed. And then it led to all kinds of harassment. Any student group was supposed to have an advisor, space on campus in the student union, and some money. UFLAGS had no advisor, no space, no money; they got harassed. The fraternities always put their banners up outside the student union where all the activities went on. When UFLAGS put up a banner, someone changed it to "UFAGS." The student group got discouraged, gave up and went off campus.

In 1986, three of us from the dean of students' office realized we really needed to do something proactively. That's when we decided we would just form this committee on our own, the Committee on Sexism and Homophobia. At the dean of students' office, we could do most anything because nobody paid attention to what we did. It wasn't a university committee, and nobody was surprised that we put "sexism" in there. They just kind of ignored the "homophobia" part. That turned out to be smart on our part. (I don't think they even knew what the word *homophobia* meant!)

Our main purpose in forming this committee was to get the student group to come back on campus, but we knew we needed to do a lot of other things mainly with fraternities, and just sensitize people on campus. We began doing all kinds of outreach, presentations, brochures, surveys, and worked with faculty.

One of the things holding everything back was that the University's antidiscrimination policy did not include homophobia. We had to change that. We were just about ready. I had asked members of the student senate if they would be in favor of that, and they were. I was just about to meet with the UF president when the State Board of Regents came down with a policy saying that no university could have a campus-wide policy that dealt with sexual orientation. So that was that. We had to move on.

We proposed making our LGBT Concerns Committee a university-wide committee to include issues that affected gay and lesbian faculty as well as students. We found a sympathetic provost to approach, but he kept dragging his feet. We had to badger him until finally he said, "Okay, okay. I'll set it up."

As a university committee, any faculty person could apply to it. The provost's secretary was interested in what we were doing because her brother was gay. She called me and said, "Let me tell you the names of people who already have applied, and you tell me whether or not you would like this person on the committee." That was great! We were able to stack it, really. The first chair was from psychology, and he was great. As a straight male, he had a lot of credibility. The whole point was to have a mix of gay, lesbian, and sympathetic straight people. That group has just done wonders. It still exists.

Still, we could not get sexual orientation added to the antidiscrimination policy. We had a very large survey of faculty and staff, which indicated that lesbians and gay men were hesitant to come out because they knew they could be fired. We had the survey, the evidence.

That was in 2003, I believe. It took us that long.

Phyllis Meek.

FROM OXFORD, MISSISSIPPI, TO ATLANTA, GEORGIA: A BLACK LESBIAN'S JOURNEY TO COMMUNITY

An Interview with Mary Anne Adams

Lorraine Fontana (LF): It is December 22, 2015. We are here at the home of Mary Anne Adams in East Point, Georgia. I'm Lorraine Fontana, who will be interviewing Mary Anne for the Womonwrites Southern Lesbian Feminist Activist Herstory Project. So, Mary Anne, I guess we should start with your background in terms of your family—where you were born, your family, and growing up.

Mary Anne Adams (MA): I was born and raised in Oxford, Mississippi, founded on land that was originally owned by the Chickasaw. I was born on September 25, 1954, just a stone's throw away from the University of Mississippi. I am one of ten children, five boys and five girls. I am the second child in the birth order, and the oldest girl. I came of age roughly in the late '60s, early '70s, and grew up in a very poor family. My mother dropped out of high school in tenth grade to care for her chronically ill grandmother. Consequently, with such a limited education, she could only find work doing menial jobs like domestic work, ironing, cooking, and occasionally picking and chopping cotton.

I was a very introverted child, very shy, with limited social skills. I was a bookworm and really didn't go outside and play with the neighborhood kids much. I was just one of those kids who had a lot of angst early on, who sat around with adults and listened to their conversations.

LF: Say something more about—while you were still in Mississippi—how you got involved in any kind of community activity, and the social justice kind of folks that you got to know.

MA: I was reared in a community called Freedman's Town. It was a community where emancipated Blacks first settled in the late 1860s, during and after the end of the Civil War. It was within walking distance of the town square and probably a mile from the University of Mississippi. Freedman's town was the center of Black culture, religion, education, and business. Due to Jim Crow, African Americans were only able to buy homes in Freedman's town, so everyone of all incomes lived in the same community. The preacher lived next to the teacher who lived next to the janitor who lived next to the mechanic. I think for the children of the community it was really a godsend, because we benefited from the diversity.

I was always a reader. I would read anything I could get my hands on and was impacted early on by the writings of Black writers, notably Gwendolyn Brooks, James Baldwin, Langston Hughes, Margaret Walker, Lorraine Hansberry, Alice Walker, Angela Davis, and Nikki Giovanni. My aunt taught high school and provided a really rich education for me. It was at her house that I listened to classical music for the first time and was introduced to a wide range of literature. I started reading *Essence Magazine* in 1970 at age sixteen when the first issue was published. It shaped my feminist views in ways both large and small. It had an emphasis on race and politics and introduced some brilliant Black women writers to the public. The early '70s were ripe with feminist teachings for me. Toni Morrison wrote her first book, *The Bluest Eye*, looking at how Black women and girls internalize white standards of beauty. Angela Davis, arrested in 1970, was singularly the most famous revolutionary Black woman of her time. *Ms. Magazine* first hit the newsstands around 1972 when I was in college at the University of Mississippi, and Alice Walker was one of the editors and also wrote her first book, *The Third Life of Grange Copeland*. I don't recall knowing any Black women role models who identified as feminist. But immersing myself in all of these magazines and books, I saw Black women who were leading, who were in *charge* of things, and I wanted to be like them. It's important to note that I saw women in the community, Black women who were in charge of things—

and by *things*, I mean institutions. Ms. Nancy Humphrey ran the Black library because we couldn't go to the white library at that time. I saw my teachers and the women in church really running things.

LF: Did you ever have a sense of being a feminist or womanist, or was your identity so tied to the Black community and issues of civil rights that feminism wasn't something you were ready to . . .

MA: That's a great question. I absolutely had the sense of being a feminist. I always questioned why boys could do certain things and girls couldn't. I questioned that early on because I just couldn't understand it. I didn't understand why every night I would pray for a bicycle for Christmas, and I never got one, but my brother had two or three bicycles. I didn't understand why, if my brother was not home, my mother would put his food in the oven, but if my sister or I were not home—oh, too bad—we had to fend for ourselves. I never understood why I had to wash dishes and my brother didn't. I didn't understand why I had to sweep the floor and he didn't because he was a boy. I questioned that always. Nobody ever explained it to me sufficiently so that I understood it. I very much started identifying as a feminist when I was in tenth, eleventh, twelfth grade. I was still very much Black-identified. I didn't have any role models really, any Black women talking to me about feminism in my community. They were talking to me through news, through magazines, you know, through TV, through books, but not face to face. I would say, probably, if I had to rank it, it would be Black and then feminist, because I was enmeshed in this Black culture, in this African American culture with all these Black men, who were certainly sexist, who were chauvinist (there's no doubt of that), but who also—because I was smart—nurtured me.

LF: Why Atlanta? What made you decide to move here?

MA: Chasing a woman. I met a woman who was in graduate school at Emory.

LF: Now we have to go back, because now you've brought out the other aspect, which is something we want to look at—knowing who you were in terms of your sexual orientation, when that happened, and when you came out, and all that kind of stuff.

MA: Well, I never had any emotional connection with men. I had boyfriends all through school; I developed physically very early, so I got the attention of men and boys early, and it was really unwanted attention. I would get catcalls and disrespectful chatter. I always had boyfriends, but I just never felt emotionally connected.

LF: Did you have any names for girls or women who were thought to be gay?

MA: In my community, no one talked about sexuality. They didn't talk about sexual orientation. They didn't talk about any of that. They didn't, even in college. There were a lot of gay guys in college, but nobody ever talked about it. I don't remember anybody talking about anything. When I was nineteen, even before I fell in love with a woman, I came to the realization that I was a lesbian. I didn't act on my feelings until years later and met a woman who turned me on to the lesbian arts community and broadened my scope of queer writers. I learned about a lot of activist LGBT folks through the *Gay Community News*! I was also part of the Southern Rural Women's Network, in Jackson, MS, at that time.

LF: Why don't you talk more about how you got to Atlanta and how you connected with the community here—in what ways. And also, what did you know about what already existed here, not only in the Black LGBT community, but did you know about ALFA [Atlanta Lesbian Feminist Alliance], which was kind of still functioning, and about AALGA [African American Lesbian Gay Alliance], and any other organizations that existed?

MA: When I came to Atlanta, I knew I wanted to be a part of the Black lesbian community. That was very important to me. I'd never really seen a group of Black lesbians, although I did come to Atlanta when Spelman had a national women's conference. Marlene Johnson was doing a workshop on the lesbian movement, Black lesbians, and I remember I could not wait to go to that workshop [laughter] because that was my first opportunity to be in a room with Black lesbians, period.

LF: What year was that?

MA: Let's see, I moved here in '88, so it was '80-something. I remember being so emotionally full, feeling this palpable connection, feeling something I never quite felt before. That day, in that room, it was as though the melding of everything I had read about, and listened to on radio and on tape, came together. I felt that for the first time I was able to be myself. I don't think I gave voice to anything that day, but I felt as though I could be safe. I was able to take that energy, and that affirmation, with me to the next step on my journey.

Somewhere around the early '90s, I connected with ZAMI: Atlanta's Premiere Organization for Lesbians of African Descent. I worked on the monthly newsletter with Lisa Moore, Anjail Rashad, later became board chair and executive director. We met monthly in women's homes, at Charis Books & More, and eventually rented an office of our own. We were very out, very visible, very political. We had a truce with some of the women—who were unable to live their lives out—that we would be the face of ZAMI, and they would be behind us, supporting us, because they feared for their safety, their jobs, their employment, their family relationships, and we did not.

LF: Do you remember what year that was?

MA: I do, because '95 was when I started the Audre Lorde Scholarship Fund, so I would say '92, '93, '94—early '90s. We were very vibrant, very active, running three to four support groups, hosting cultural events, marching in parades, locally and nationally. It was very important for us to create visibility of Black lesbians, to be politicized, to push our way to the table.

LF: Would you say ZAMI ever had a particular culture, whether it be literary or arts or music? I know you had the scholarship fund, which is educational.

MA: Yes, we were absolutely literary, cultural, social, political—everything we did was intersectional. What we saw, in terms of the media in Atlanta, who were speaking for us, were white gay men primarily, and we wanted to say, this is who we are. We have a voice. We're part of this community. And one way to do that, in terms of visibility, was to put on those cultural events.

We published a monthly newsletter and were the first group to bring Sharon Bridgforth here, and also Michelle Parkerson and Ada Gay Griffin, to screen Audre Lorde's film *Litany for Survival*. The first fundraiser we ever had, Jocelyn Taylor, who was a filmmaker in New York City at the time, came and brought a series of her short films. We were at Emory to screen that. We knew that it would be strategic for us to be able to do that, to bring people together around art and music and song that was nonthreatening. It was a way for people to learn more about lesbian herstory and culture. These folks we would bring were very political people, and they were Black lesbians. We brought Nikky Finney, CC Carter. It was amazing. We would also partner with Charis Books & More, the local feminist bookstore, to sponsor readings. We were very intentional in creating that kind of culture.

LF: Did you get support from the [white-controlled] LGBT news media to get that information out to people?

MA: Yes, they absolutely wanted to cover us, and they *did* do that. We were also able to have Charis make announcements for us. We would utilize their space a lot. We certainly utilized the First E—we felt that was our home. Lanier [Rev. Lanier Clance, who was the founding minister of First Existentialist Congregation of Atlanta at that time] was just absolutely supportive.

I think one of the other things we were able to do, as an organization, was to do a lot of coalition work, I think more than any other organization actually. We were able to get a grant from Astraea to bring in the students from the AU [Atlanta University] Center. We brought them into Atlanta two Saturdays a month. We hired a program manager because they said to us that they felt unsafe on campus. A lot of people don't know that. They were able to talk and connect with each other around issues that were impacting them.

LF: Did that help them create Afrekete?

MA: Actually, this was a little before. Wendy O'Neil and Antonia Randolph started the Lesbian and Bisexual Student Alliance on Spelman campus, and they did talk with me about that, prior to them starting LBSA, absolutely. Lilly Huddleston and Kathi Williams were partners at the time, and they had a little jazz joint we would use. We were also able to get a grant to have a program called "Building Bridges" with other lesbians of color. We would do that once a month. We would have big dinners that "A Time to Dine" Pepper and Michelle would cater.

Mary Anne Adams.

It's also important to mention that Fourth Tuesday Atlanta, Atlanta Health Initiative, and Women's Outdoor Network partnered two years in a row (c. 1999–2000) to host a basketball tournament, with the proceeds going to ZAMI's Audre Lorde Scholarship Fund.

LF: Was there a continuous ZAMI presence through the present time?

MA: Absolutely. We continued to grow and evolve. We put on the first drag king show in the city. We did that during Black Gay Pride for a number of years. It was our big annual fundraising event, and people really looked forward to it. It was huge.

ELEANOR SMITH: DISABILITY ACTIVIST
From an interview by Dancingwater[1]

I moved to Georgia from Indiana in 1972 to volunteer at Koinonia, a Christian communal farm established in 1942. I wanted to live in an intentional community and had been drawn to their liberal politics and commitment to service. Koinonia subscribed to progressive periodicals from around the world for their small library. One day in 1973 while I was reading *The Great Speckled Bird*, a counterculture newspaper based in Atlanta, I saw an article and photo of the Red Dyke Theatre.[2] I already identified as a lesbian and got very excited that a population of left-leaning, lesbian-identified women was only a couple of hours away. When I decided to leave Koinonia after a year and a half, that memory of Atlanta beckoned to me. The warm weather was also a plus, as at that time there was not much awareness about accessibility or infrastructure to support living independently in a wheelchair, and I knew I would not do well with snow-ridden city streets.

Before I decided to move, I sent a letter to the Atlanta Lesbian Feminist Alliance, ALFA, asking for information about the lesbian community. I was delighted when I received a handwritten letter from Lorraine Fontana welcoming me. That letter convinced me Atlanta would be where I would live next. One of the great services that ALFA historically performed was connecting lesbian women all over the South with community, visibility, and pride.

The first performance I saw in Atlanta turned out to be the Red Dyke Theatre. There were over 100 lesbians together in one

---

1 Dancingwater interviewed Eleanor Smith at her home in Atlanta in spring 2016. This was not a recorded interview, so was not archived.

2 See Merril Mushroom, "Red Dyke Theatre," *Sinister Wisdom* 104 (2017): 135–38.

room, and my head was spinning with amazement. So many women! And the performers were talented and funny.

I got involved in ALFA immediately. At that time you had to climb up three steps to enter the space. I would drive my car to the ALFA house a little early—a hand-controlled car where I folded up the wheelchair and put it behind the driver's seat—so that women coming to the same meeting could lift me in my chair up to the entrance. One time when I arrived late, I picked up stones and pinged them at the window till someone came out. ALFA membership paid for materials, and women built a ramp in 1982 so that there would be no hindrance to women in chairs. I remember cutting the ribbon at the ramp celebration. Lesbians have always been ahead of the curve—relatively speaking—in providing access to events through ramps, American Sign Language translations, and engaging the issues of racism, sexism, and homophobia.

The first ALFA committee I joined was the newsletter, which provided information about news and events relevant to lesbian-identified women throughout the South. I would write articles and help put out the newsletter. We had workdays/parties where we would crank out over 100 newsletters, collate, staple, and address them. I wrote articles about the opening of the feminist bookstore Charis Books (1974) and my trip to the 2nd Michigan Womyn's Music Festival (1977). I also wrote an etiquette guide for straight women when meeting lesbians, meant to be humorous and educational. One of the lines was "If you must back away, do so slowly."[3]

I marched with ALFA under our banner in the Lesbian and Gay Pride Parade in 1975 and for several years after that. When I think back on that 1975 event today, I remember that some folks

---

[3] After the interview, Eleanor Smith reported that she had Googled that line and discovered that over the years the etiquette guide has shown up in more than forty books and magazines, in every case misattributing its source. The most recent is included in a women's studies anthology published in 2017, *Women in Culture: An Intersectional Anthology for Gender and Women's Studies*, 2nd Edition.

marched with paper bags over their heads. There was absolutely no job protection in those days, and people were often fired if employers found out they were lesbian or gay. Marching without the bag, I felt nervous. I worked for the state of Georgia then and was worried I would stand out in my wheelchair and be identified and fired. I have the utmost respect for all the folks who showed up with bags over their heads at that time. They paved the way for the bagless marching of today.

ALFA gave us an opportunity not just to advocate for lesbian and feminist issues but also to create. In 1980 and '81 I had been on an extended stay in San Francisco for a counseling training program, and there I sang in the women's chorus. When I returned to Atlanta, I initiated a lesbian singing group at the ALFA house. For several months we just sang together from mimeographed sheets with no director, and then Judy Aehle found our first musical director, Linda Vaughn.[4] We sang music about peace, freedom, and self-pride. I remember performing at our first concert, with only about a dozen singers, for ALFA's tenth birthday party in 1982. We sang "What I Did for Love" and "Amelia Earhart." Walking around the room after the performance, I noticed tears in more than one woman's eyes when they said they liked the performance. I had the feeling they were feeling, "Lesbians aren't just surviving, we're creating! We have a chorus!" It felt so good to be part of something artistic that had the power to create both joy and community.

The first lesbian music concert I attended took place in one of the earliest lesbian gathering places in Atlanta, the Tower Lounge. Meg Christian, touring for Olivia records, performed, in 1975 or '76, I believe, with the audience crowded together sitting on the floor, whooping and hollering as she sang "Ode to a Gym Teacher" and "Here Come the Lesbians." In later years, after Chris Carroll and others started Lucina's Music, I attended a lot of the high-energy concerts they produced.

---

4 See Charlene Ball, "Atlanta Feminist Women's Chorus," *Sinister Wisdom* 104 (2017): 61–68.

Another connection was with Karuna Counseling for Women and Their Friends. When I first came to town, I read in *Creative Loafing* about that newly formed organization. I was feeling very anxious, not having a job yet and not knowing anyone well. I really needed help, so I called Karuna and became a client. I was lucky to find this organization, still existing today, whose founding group were mostly lesbians. Later, returning from training in California, I worked at Karuna as a counselor for four years.

Eleanor Smith, Atlanta, 1974.

INFORM, INSPIRE, CONNECT: FIVE YEARS WITH *THE NEWSLETTER*

Laurel Ferejohn

I was thirty-six and about to be divorced when a colleague at Duke read between my lines and gave me a copy of *The Newsletter*—"a monthly newsletter and biweekly calendar for all lesbians and feminist women" of our area, the back cover said.[1] The year was 1986, and the women's community in Durham, North Carolina—underground as it was—was in full swing, as I was about to find out.

The Newsletter was a revelation. I'd been here for three years but knew nothing about local lesbian community. And I was working on a feminist journal at Duke! Mostly my cluelessness was the result of my own shyness—possibly fear—but also the community did a great job of existing *underground*.

Once I had *The Newsletter* in my hands, I still couldn't figure out who anyone was. All the names—the coordinators, the bylines on articles—were first name plus initial. Lucky for me, my friend continued to make it easy. She let me tag along to events, starting with a dance at the YWCA. My jaw dropped and my heart rose: Women everywhere! Dancing! Together! That was the most exciting moment of my life up to then. I met my first girlfriend that night, who just happened to be a *Newsletter* coordinator. I became one, too.

The underground-ness continued—first name and initial, no public distribution of copies, no external advertising for subscriptions—only now I was part of that underground, 500 subscribers and counting. The underground-ness definitely had

---

1   See also Nancy Blood, Leslie Kahn, Donna Giles, Sherry Kinlaw, Sherri Zann Rosenthal, Cynthie Kulstad, Patience Vanderbush, and Dee Lutz, "Triangle Area Newsletter Memories," *Sinister Wisdom* 116 (2020): 127–32.

its upside, because once a woman did find *The Newsletter*, she could feel safe that she wouldn't necessarily be outing herself by being on the mailing list. At the time I'm talking about—mid-'80s to -'90s—as we know, it could still be really risky to be out.

For example, when I was arrested in a 1989 civil disobedience around Senator Jesse Helms's horrific stance on AIDS, I came very close to being fired from my job over it. My job was with a *medical* journal, whose business manager saw anything having to do with AIDS as all about *homosexuals*. His approach to me was what we now might call a #MeToo experience. Things could get ugly in some quarters if it was even *suspected*, by *association*, that you *might* be a *lesbian*.

Right around that same time, in 1989, we *Newsletter* coordinators made the decision to end the no-last-names-permitted policy. Now everyone would have a choice about it. That first issue, with "Laurel Ferejohn" where "Laurel F." used to be, was like a coming of age. Maybe it felt like that to others, too; very few women opted for the initial.

Then the name policy came under *re*consideration. One Saturday I picked up the mail from *The Newsletter*'s PO box and found a handwritten letter from what appeared to be a Klan terrorist threatening a "race war" (his words). My thought was to give the letter to Mab Segrest, then head of North Carolinians against Racist and Religious Violence. She knew right away who the letter writer was, by name, even though there was no name on it. This was really reassuring—not to have it confirmed that this guy was in fact a card-carrying terrorist, but that someone had a bead on him.

As coordinators we were concerned that he had found the PO address. Did he get it from a copy of *The Newsletter*? Did he have our full names? We didn't change course on the policy, though; nothing further happened, and most of us kept on using full names.

Over this five-year period circulation topped 1,000, and scores of topics were explored in *The Newsletter*'s pages, like the silent vigil for a Klan march (1986), Durham's antidiscrimination ordinance (1987), k.d. lang (1989). Alongside many amazing women, I became involved as a volunteer with several progressive organizations, marched in the marches, got arrested, and served on the board of Our Own Place, lesbian space in Durham,[2] all of it reported in the pages of our community newsletter.

I moved to a different part of the state in 1991 and left *The Newsletter*. It had by then served for ten continuous years as a key community-building and organizing tool. It had informed, inspired, and connected us to each other through a tumultuous decade. I'm grateful to have been involved for five of those years.

---

2 Laurel Ferejohn, "Organizing Our Own Place: Durham, NC," *Sinister Wisdom* 109 (2018): 77–81.

INSPIRED TO HONOR WOMONWRITERS WHO HAD PASSED

Drea Firewalker

Today I sit quietly listening to the raindrops hitting the tin roof of my art studio, reflecting on the rituals I was inspired to create to honor the passion and the wisdom of deceased lesbians who once participated in Womonwrites: the Southeast Lesbian Writers Conference, a conference I, too, have attended for many years. Myriad changes in the philosophy of what it is to be lesbian, thus who could attend the conference, caused it to divide after forty years. This pending loss must have prompted the spirits of some of the early founding and sustaining Womonwriters to make contact with me and ask for tributes to their early visions of a lesbian writing conference, and now to their crone souls.

Voices Fall 2017

This is how my inspiration came for creating the first memorial installation at the Womonwrites conference. The spirits of former Womonwriters, many of whom I had not known, came to me in my dreams. When I was sleeping, I was aware that I was resting beyond the veil in the spirit world. When the spirits woke me, I felt their energy. I could sense their words like a soft breath: "Not this time, not this time." I had been planning to facilitate another croning celebration at the conference. I realized I had to postpone it. Their voices like whispers in the beginning became stronger: "We are the crones, crones." I heard them declare that they wanted to be brought back into the circle of the current Womonwriters to be acknowledged as past participants and to be honored in their present form as crone spirits. I was to speak their names out loud and create a ritual for them.

I created an artistic installation in a large, open area outside the conference meeting rooms. I gathered a list of thirty names and obtained most of their pictures from different Womonwriters. I was instructed to drive thirty wooden staffs into the ground to create a circular border and place a staff to honor each deceased Womonwriter. These staffs represented the connection to mother earth and the Womonwriters' bonds in death to each other and to us.

Inside the circle of staffs, I placed thirty chairs in a staggered pattern and covered them with purple fabric. I placed a picture of a deceased Womonwriter on each chair with a candle in front of the picture. I lit a pathway to the center altar to fold them all into the light. I encouraged all women at the conference to enter the circle any time and held a special ritual on Saturday night.

Remembrance circle at Womonwrites 2017. Womonwrites readings and workshops were often held in the building in the background, which we named Adrienne Rich.

When the last stories of the conference were read, I read from the stage the name of each woman who had passed away. After the last name, I saw the spirits of the Womonwriters move back into the ethers to wait for us to honor them. Phyllis Free drummed and Sarah Salamander danced her healing dance as current Womonwriters gathered outside the circle of chairs and then entered, one by one, and lit a candle in front of a deceased writer's picture and said that woman's name out loud. After all thirty candles had been lit, there was an incredibly powerful pull of emotions by the living and dead as each remembered one another. Quiet fell on the group. I felt the departed Womonwriters' pleasure at our seeing them among us. They had been there all weekend.

Voices Spring 2018

The Womonwriters who had died asked very little of me to honor them for the spring 2018 gathering. I understood they had begun their own separation from the land and the other living Womonwriters. The memorial would be simple. A small circle held each deceased Womonwriter's name on a lavender scarf. This year there were thirty-three. Salamander had offered to dance part of the healing ritual for holding the women together.

When I set up the sacred space for the ritual, the energy in the air seemed extremely heavy, as if the sky would weep tears. Indeed, it had rained, and although the names had been written in permanent dye, the ink ran and began to fade the women's names. I was so shaken by the sight, I hurriedly restored each of the thirty-three women's names to the scarves.

At the conference, tension continued over whether to include in the conference anyone who called herself a lesbian, and the afternoon readings turned into bickering. Afterward, the Womonwriters walked right past the sacred space where the ritual was to be held and into the dining hall. The deceased Womonwriters to be honored were invisible to them. Only five Womonwriters stood to speak their goodbyes in the now broken circle. There would be no remembering their names or recalling their stories. Very few women stopped at the memorial during the conference. Later I would wrap up the wet scarves and gather the staffs with barely a glance from Womonwriters torn with division on the dining hall porch.

Photo by Leaf Cronewrite

Remembrance Circle at Womonwrites, spring 2018. The dining hall in the background was known to us as Radclyffe Hall.

Voices Fall 2018

I had numerous visits again from those who had died, sometimes dancing, waving ribbons, or speaking boldly about honoring them at Womonwrites by displaying their images. They chose a wall in the dining hall that had been used for years for workshop announcements. I had little sleep for a number of nights as I argued with them about the placement. They held firm that I would secure the space for them.

The first day of the conference I was surprised that the coordinators offered little resistance to my request. On the big open wall in the dining hall, I placed a picture of each Womonwriter on a large purple cloth extending from the floor to ceiling. Inside

I placed long strips of white paper in a V shape to name the memorial, and in the center of the V a lighted labrys. This display was to remind the Womonwriters that our deceased forerunners were still among us. As some of us gathered for meals or games near the wall, we did remember their stories and talk about their life journeys. There were more images of deceased Womonwriters on the wall than living Womonwriters attending this smallest fall gathering.

Courtesy of Drea Firewalker

Firewalker stands next to the Remembrance Wall at Fall Womonwrites 2018.

Voices January 2019

The spirit voices of the deceased Womonwriters grew quiet. I thought those from the other side were comforted by the memorials I created. But early in 2019, the dreams and voices began again. Miriam was dancing naked into my dreams. She was light and clear as she spoke to me. She was twirling among the grass and the plants. Her voice echoed, "Do you see me," not in a questioning tone, but emphatically. She knew she had my full attention. She said, "Now breathe deeply. Others will come to direct you." I gathered four more names and pictures of deceased Womonwriters to be honored.

At their request, I set up three canopies, each with a different representation: Reflections, Remembrances, Reconnections. Beneath each canopy, I placed a group of deceased Womonwriters' pictures upright on the ground in a half-moon circle. Around each canopy, I placed staffs, attached to each staff a purple scarf bearing their names. Within and around the canopies were tree branches. In the beginning, the trees were seeds. Out of the ashes will be decay, which will then feed mother earth to start a new cycle for all. I asked Beth York to sing in the presence of the canopies so that the ground was gifted by a vocal healing vibration and clearing of the space.

I invited all current Womonwriters into this sacred space to honor the thirty-seven Womonwriters who had walked the land, swam the lake, and stood and shared their stories in previous conferences. An altar was set at the entrance of each canopy. Women could add a token of honor on any altar. One chair in each canopy faced the half-moon circle of pictures so women could sit and speak from their heart to the spirits. A current Womonwriter crone guardian was also standing under each canopy. In the center, between the three canopies, a cauldron holding lake water was set to receive pieces of paper women inscribed and released after igniting with a candle. Women could release anything, hopes or dreams, to leave with the Womonwriters who have passed and with the land.

How powerful the ground around me had felt as I prepared and built the honoring space. I remembered how each candle, staff, picture, and name placed on a scarf was done, and how the spirits wished their pictures to be placed next to another crone spirit they were at peace with. I didn't know that these rituals would be releasing them from the land where this Womonwrites conference had been held for forty years. Ironically, no Womonwriters would gather on this land again since the conference would cease to exist after this spring.

On the last day of the last Womonwrites conference, May 19, 2019, those deceased Womonwriters spoke to me. "Get up. The dew is rising from the ground. We are leaving." By the time I had reached the three canopies in the memorial area, I knew some of the spirits had already left. I watched as the sun broke the beads of water on the light air. I watched as the spirits, one by one, left the land. I wept, not for them leaving, but for what they had given me, the strength to honor their passion for Womonwrites and their wisdom. Watching them leave, I wondered if they would speak again to inspire lesbian writers to gather? If they do, this crone knows how to listen.

Memorial with Firewalker's crone drawing at Womonwrites 2019, the last Womonwrites.

Photo by Lorraine Fontana

THESE FRIENDS OF MINE

Lyrics by Lenny Lasater and Mendy Knott
Music by Lenny Lasater

© BMI 2010

G　　　　　G　　　　　　　　　　C
These friends of mine they're with me all the time
　　　　　　　　　　　　　　　D
Feeling sad or feeling fine, when it rains or if it shines
　　　　　　　　　　G　　(B-C-C#-D)
These friends are mine
　　　　　　　　　　　　　　　　　G
There're even with me when they're gone
　　　　　　　　　　　　　C　　　　　　　　D
cause no matter where we roam I'm never far from home
　　　　　　　　　　　　　　　　　　　　　　G
And I know I ain't alone with these friends of mine
F　　　　　　　　　　C　　　　　　G　　　　　　C
We've seen lovers come and go sometimes fast but mostly slow
　　　　　　　　　G　　　　　C　　　D
When I'm really feeling low　all I need to know is
　　　　　　　　　　　　　G　　　　　　　　　　　C
That these friends of mine are with me all the time
　　　　　　　　　　　　D
They help me hold the line and get through the daily grind
　　　　　　　　　　　　　　　G
I need these friends of mine
F　　　　　　　　　　　　　C
You know in these past few years
　　　　　　G　　　　　　　　　　C　　　　　　G　　　　　　C
We've faced our share of fears　Lord we cried a million tears

```
D
But those ole grey skies seem to clear
                G                            C
With these friends of mine they're with me all the time
              D
I'm the singer they're the rhyme and I don't need another sign
                        G      (B-C-C#-D)
Not with these friends of mine
            G              C
These friends of mine they're with me all the time
              D
We walk a long thin line and I got Cherry on my mind
                  G
I need these friends of mine
                D
I don't need another sign I'm so grateful for this time
                G
With these friends of mine
```

WRITING "THESE FRIENDS OF MINE"

Lenny Lasater

I was honored to be Cherry Omega's power of attorney in 2005 during her final days with us. Managing the mountain of paperwork to secure an early retirement settlement from a large trade union and insurance companies was quite a task. It seemed all I did was shuttle back and forth from Atlanta to North Carolina to shove documents under her nose for signatures. That left me little time to visit and connect with her. After her passing on June 28, 2005, I was left feeling that I had missed the most precious moments I could have spent with her.

In early September 2005, right after Katrina had blown through, I was at a Mary Gauthier concert. Her music was powerful and resonated with me. She talked about coming to songwriting later in life. She said, "Write about what you know. Keep it simple. You're not Joni Mitchell after all!"

I had sung in the Atlanta Feminist Women's Chorus and entertained the idea of being in a band, but had never tried to write a song. Being more of a "music" person than a "lyric" person, I thought it unlikely I would ever be a songwriter. That night after Mary's concert, Cherry Omega came to me in my dreams. I was awakened with the melody and a rough draft of lyrics for "These Friends of Mine." I jumped up and scribbled down the words on a dry-cleaning ticket as the tune played over and over in my head. And wouldn't ya know, it's a waltz!

Cherry Omega spoke so clearly to me in my dream. She thanked me for being her friend, and for all the work I had done. She reminded me of all the others who had propped me up during that time. Later, I worked with Mendy Knott to fashion the words into the lyrics of the song.

In June 2006, I got sober, and soon started the Americana/alt-country band Roxie Watson.[1] "These Friends of Mine" was one of the first songs Roxie recorded. Today, the trio Just Roxie still performs this song, and it has become one of our most requested. This song is a tribute to all the people, friends, loved ones, the "village," if you will, needed to help us get through life, the good times and the bad.

Thank you, Cherry "O," for haunting my dreams as you still do today. I feel you near me so often. I miss you every day, Buddy.

---

[1] The Roxie Watson Band is now Just Roxie, but you can still listen to "These Friends of Mine" on YouTube with band members Lenny Lasater, bass; Beth Wheeler, mandolin; Linda Bolley, acoustic and electric guitar; Sonia Tetlow, banjo; Becky Shaw, button accordion, harmonica, lap steel, acoustic guitar. All sing vocals. Their debut album, with "These Friends of Mine," was *True Stories* (2010). Their music is available on iTunes, Amazon Music, etc. See also ourstage.com/epk/roxiewatson.

THE SOUTHERN LESBIAN FEMINIST ACTIVIST HERSTORY COLLECTION IN *SINISTER WISDOM*

This edition of *Sinister Wisdom* marks the sixth and final special issue in the series devoted to Southern lesbian-feminist herstory. In 2009, a group of lesbian writers gathered under the pines at Womonwrites: the Southeast Lesbian Writers Conference to discuss the preservation of our rich herstory. Many of us recognized that the lesbian-feminist voices of Southern lesbians had been omitted or marginalized in mainstream literature of the LGBTQ movement as well as from feminist history. We committed to preserving the activism of lesser-known Southern lesbians during the second wave of feminism from 1968 to 1994, and soon our timeline stretched to the end of the century. For the first three years, we did not know where the project was going, and it was not until 2012 that we stopped soliciting memoirs (which we were not getting) and started recording interviews, which made the project really take off. About that time, Beth York and Rose Norman made a research trip to the Sallie Bingham Center for Women's History and Culture at Duke University to see where those archives might lead us. They found a treasure trove of material about the Atlanta Lesbian Feminist Alliance (ALFA) and Atlanta's Charis Books, as well as wonderful materials about Womonwrites in the archives of two of the cofounders, Minnie Bruce Pratt and Mab Segrest. That research trip led to Womonwrites turning over a huge collection of material previously stored in a garage (https://archives.lib.duke.edu/catalog/womonwrites). By then, we were calling ourselves "The Herstory Project," with a nod to the Lesbian Herstory Archives in Brooklyn. The Sallie Bingham Center, being in the South and already archiving Southern lesbian-feminists, soon became the obvious place for archiving our interviews. Those interviews are now a subset of the Womonwrites archive (https://archives.lib.duke.edu/catalog/slfaherstoryproject).

A turning point came when Barbara Ester asked, "Why don't we contact *Sinister Wisdom*?" Barb had been published in an issue on music and the arts and thought that the editors of *Sinister Wisdom* would be interested in our project. Barbara was right. And so began our relationship with *Sinister Wisdom* editor Julie Enszer, a relationship that has guided and shaped our project ever since. Our project grew from a handwritten timeline of remembered events and organizations to a time when Womonwriters began to commit to writing about those topics. With the leadership and expertise of Rose Norman and Merril Mushroom, *Sinister Wisdom* published the first special issue, *Southern Lesbian Feminist Herstory, 1968–1994* (SW 93, Summer 2014). In the process of creating that first issue, we realized that the project was flowering from what we had thought would be one issue to three, then four, now six. Julie Enszer enthusiastically encouraged us to continue. Issues followed on *Landykes of the South* (SW 98, Fall 2015); lesbian-feminist arts (*Lesbianima Rising*, SW 104, Spring 2017); lesbian spaces (*HotSpots: Creating Lesbian Space in the South*, SW 109, Summer 2018); *Making Connections* (SW 116, Spring 2020), honoring bookstores, publishers, newsletters, and the byways through which lesbian literature was distributed throughout the South; and this final issue on our spiritual and political paths, which we view as one.

The project has been intensely collaborative and geographically dispersed. The nine editors of these six issues live in five Southern states and have communicated primarily through email, plus three times a year in person at Womonwrites conferences and Womonwrites planning weekends (through 2019). Rose Norman and Merril Mushroom, who have worked on all six issues, live about two hours apart, in Alabama and Tennessee, respectively. Kate Ellison and Barbara Esrig, who have each worked on two issues, live fairly near each other in Florida. Beth York, who has also worked on two issues, lives in South Carolina. B. Leaf Cronewrite, Gail Reeder, and Lorraine Fontana all live in the Atlanta area. Robin Toler, whose art graces all six covers of these issues, lives in Louisiana. All of these, and many more, have worked tirelessly to find more and more stories as themes emerged that took us well beyond our original idea of collecting stories from people we knew and their friends.

Rose Norman began to travel, first interviewing lesbians in Gainesville, FL, and Atlanta, then reaching out to Durham, NC, which brought in many stories of Triangle Area lesbianfeminists. Merril Mushroom's suggestion that we contact Beth Marschak in Richmond, VA, brought in a whole new set of lesbian-feminist activists, as we found more and more "hot spots" beyond Atlanta and Gainesville, which were already familiar to us. Rather than simply recording interviews and archiving them, we began mining the interviews for more polished stories. In that vein, Phyllis Free turned Rose Norman's six separate interviews with Southerners on New Ground founders into one interview, as if they had been interviewed together. Even though we were cutting down long interviews into shorter stories, we often struggled to fit a wealth of stories into the limits of a single issue. Mercifully, Julie Enszer often let us exceed our word limit.

We are deeply grateful to Julie Enszer and the volunteer editors and contributors that have made this collection possible. We count at least eighty lesbians who have submitted stories, poetry, and song. Even more lesbians have been interviewed, and those transcripts have been preserved in the Sallie Bingham Center for Women's History and Culture in the David M. Rubenstein Rare Book and Manuscript Library at Duke University. We will continue to collect and archive stories of lesbian-feminist activism in the South, and possibly turn some of them into stories for future open issues of *Sinister Wisdom* or for other publications. If you would like to archive your story of lesbian-feminist activism in the South, write us at SLFAherstoryproject@gmail.com. Some of the interviews are already available online at https://repository.duke.edu/dc/slfaherstoryproject. Rose Norman did so many interviews with the women of Pagoda that she is now writing a book about that lesbian-feminist intentional community and cultural center in St. Augustine, FL. Phyllis Free's "Goddess Chant" and Barb Ester's "Lover's Touch" are included on a new recording of original songs performed at Womonwrites entitled *Finding Home* (Beth York, 2019).

We are proud of our contributions to lesbian culture and strengthened by our collective voices. We enthusiastically give young Southern lesbians who read these pages many strong shoulders to stand on.

Covers from the five previous SLFAHP special issues before this one.

Project Planning at Womonwrites 2011. (l to r) Merril Mushroom, Barbara Ester, Kate Ellison, Lorraine Fontana, Harvest (Diane Boward), Gail Reeder, Reba Hood, Beth York, Phyllis Free.

The workshop at Spring 2016 Womonwrites drew a big crowd of SLFAHP collaborators. (l to r) Rand Hall, Gail Reeder, Womonwriter, Kate Ellison, Phyllis Free, Beth York, Sage Morse, Corky Culver, B. Leaf Cronewrite (and behind her) Brae Hodgkin, Drea Firewalker, Barbara Ester, Barbara Esrig, (and behind Barbara) Merril Mushroom, Woody Blue, Rose Norman, Lorraine Fontana. Almost everyone in this picture has a story in this issue.

Herstorians gather for planning at Outrageous Voices fall 2019. (l to r) Sarah Salamander Thorsen, Helen Renée Brawner, Barbara Esrig, Rose Norman, Judy McVey, Lorraine Fontana.

Herstorians gather to plan the SW116 release parties and work on SW 124 at Dykewriters, December 2019. They are holding various SW special issues that we did and the new *Sinister Wisdom* 2020 calendar that SW editor Julie Enszer had sent to everybody. (l to r) Seated: Womonwriter, Rose Norman, Kate Ellison, Woody Blue. Standing: Robin Romaine, Barbara Ester, Edie Daly, Barbara Stoll, Contributor, Phyllis Free, Beth York, Torii Black, B. Leaf Cronewrite, Gail Reeder, Trey Anderson, Debra Gish, and Sage Morse.

SNAPSHOT LESBIAN LOVE CELEBRATION

I remember Martha Shelley from the 70s lesbian feminist uprising. She is still a political activist and writes blogs and publishes with *Ebisu Publications*. She and her partner, Sylvian Allen, are honored in this segment, hoping their love stories add to your day like they did to mine. (Roberta Arnold)

About Martha, by Sylvia

I first met Martha Shelley on a strangely hot day in San Francisco in February 1997, when I was leading weekly city hikes for women. It was my Land's End hike and I had about 20 hikers. Martha was with us for the first time and behaved badly. She demanded ice cream (which she didn't get), insisted that I divert the hike to a different, much more difficult trail (which we didn't do), and finally took off her shoes and waded in the decorative fountain outside the Legion of Honor Museum. That last was actually okay with me but she also threatened to remove more garments, and I had to tell her, "No, you may NOT take your pants off." She pointed out that she had underpants on. It definitely felt like taking my two-year-old for a walk.

However, in between the bad behavior, she told me about the series of novels she was writing, set in the 9th century BCE, and we talked about Judaism and historical fiction. I enjoyed her conversation tremendously, and was amused and intrigued by the combination of childlike behavior and sparkling intellect, and the passion for justice that showed through both.

She never came back to City Hikes, but I remembered her, and months later one of my regular hikers commented, "You sure like talking about Martha Shelley."

Some months later, in October, I attended a friend's birthday party—a sit-down dinner in a restaurant—and the person who happened to sit across from me was Martha. We were both celebrating: She had just had her *Haggadah* published, and my article on communicating with people with AIDS dementia had just been accepted in a respected journal. We didn't talk to anyone else all evening. Someone down the table was talking about a movie from the film festival, "When Night Is Falling," and Martha said to me, "That was a great movie. You should rent it and watch it on your VCR."

"I don't have a VCR," I told her.

"Then you and your girlfriend should come watch it on my VCR."

"I don't have a girlfriend."

The rest is history. We're still together, 24 years later. I still love Martha for the same reasons I found her so memorable on that hot day at Land's End.

About Sylvia, by Martha

Sylvia used to lead hikes for women in San Francisco. I joined one in February 1997, and really enjoyed conversing with her. She was interested in my research on the ancient Middle East, for my novels about Jezebel. But when she left a message inviting me to another city hike, I didn't respond, preferring to tramp around the woods instead.

I met her again at the end of October, when a mutual friend invited us to a birthday party at a restaurant. We found ourselves sitting opposite each other and once again couldn't stop talking, mostly about our writing projects. Occasionally I'd tear my attention away and say a word to someone else, but it was an effort. Then, when another woman praised a lesbian flick from that year's film festival, and Sylvia said she'd missed it, I suggested she rent it. She said she didn't have a VCR—or a girlfriend to watch it with. I blurted, "Then you can see it at my place."

Next weekend we watched the movie. The following weekend we hiked the length of Ocean Beach and back, then watched the stars come out. Sylvia is taller than me, with long legs, and I struggled to keep up but was too proud to let her know that until years later. The weekend after that, we climbed the Glen Canyon Park trail. That night she seemed a lot prettier than she had before—until I realized that her looks hadn't changed. I was falling in love. I'd planned the fourth date to be an East Bay hills hike. We got all the way from my front door to the bedroom.

On Thanksgiving we drove to Point Reyes, hiked out to the beach, and ate a festive meal at the base of the waterfalls. Then we spent the night at her place. In the morning I said, "I think I'd better get my camels together"—meaning the bride price.

She understood. "I think you'd better."

Proposed and accepted. We were married (though not yet legally) in 1998.

Martha and Sylvia Sitting on Steps

BOOK REVIEW

There At The Dawning:
Memories of a Lesbian Feminist
By **Barbara J. Love**
238 pages, $15. Paperback

Reviewed by Roberta Arnold

There At The Dawning is not your everyday memoir. In it, Barbara Love combines first-hand accounts of gay and lesbian political events that shaped LGBTQ history with personal memories. Love is the co-author of *Sappho Was a Right-on Woman: A Liberated View of Lesbianism*. *There at the Dawning* begins with an anonymous letter to Barbara Love and Sydney Abbott (co-author) thanking them for their truth-telling and for reinforcing the power inherent in being a lesbian: "Thank you! Thank you! I'm still scared shitless, but I know that when the smoke clears, I'll have a much higher opinion of myself…" (1).

Beginning her life as a national championship swimmer, Love is aware of her lesbianism early on, but hides it from her upper-middle-class Republican family in Ridgewood, NJ for many years. While wending her way from the bars to the politics of second wave feminism, she begins by searching for affirmation of her lesbianism in the bar scene. Describing the demeaning and humiliating trip to the bathroom where every woman is handed four squares of toilet paper before entering a cubicle, prison life comes to mind. Love elicits the poignant depth of this moment, borrowing a quote by Joan Nestle from her book, *A Restricted Country*: "Burned deeply in our endurance was our fury. That (bathroom) line was practice and theory seared into one. We wove our freedoms, our culture around their obstacles of hatred, but we also paid our price, every time I took the fistful of toilet paper, I swore eventual liberation. It would be, however, liberation with memory" (61-62). Nestle also recounts a raid on *The Sea Colony*, the lesbian bar on the corner of 13th Street and Hudson Avenue in New York City where forty-six lesbians were arrested in 1964. This is the very same place Love begins her lesbian journey. The quotidian mistreatment of lesbians there perhaps seared into her activism; the die is cast.

Love's life is filled with action. She meets Sidney Abbott, co-author of *Sappho Was A Right-on Woman*, gets ejected from her family when she comes out to them, tries out butch-femme roles, gets badly beaten up for looking butch, finds the Quaker Gay Liberation Front meetings, becomes co-treasurer with a Marsha P. Johnson, who co-started STAR (Street Transvestites Action Revolutionaries), becomes active in NOW, and begins CR (consciousness raising) after Rita Mae Brown visits the Gay Liberation front (GLF) and invites various members to her 13th Street apartment to form Consciousness Raising groups.

Love is an excellent story-teller. She describes many of the stories we've known and read about in bursts of activity, such as the action to take over the office of the editor of *Ladies Home Journal*, the Radicalesbians, and "The Lavender Menace." Love becomes a member of the Radicalesbians, a direct offshoot of GLF, and leaves it after feeling alien to some of their ways, including not from a working-class background. "The appropriate breeding ground for a radical was working class" (p 84). She describes Abbott as being "deeply hurt" (p 84) when her father dies and no one in the group says anything to her. Then the group trashing of Kate Millet after her publication of *Sexual Politics* puts things over the top. Love thought it was vicious: "The atmosphere was permeated with an air of attack, attack, attack" (84-85). The Lesbian Menace action comes a year after the First Congress to Unite Women in 1969 which excluded lesbian groups and Betty Friedan (co-founder of NOW) referred to lesbians as 'The Lavender Menace," claiming they would detract from getting women's rights realized.

Love also gives her first-hand account and opinion of the *Woman-Identified Woman* paper: "In my opinion, this was one of the most important papers of the second wave women's movement. *Woman-Identified Woman* recognized brilliantly that lesbianism had important implications for women's liberation" (p 80). In 1972, Love, also a member of NOW and NGTF (National Gay Task Force), attends the Democratic National Convention in Miami. Shirley Chisolm was on the ballot for president. McGovern becames the party nominee, losing to Nixon by a large margin. Abbott & Love are meant to address the issue of gay rights, but their plank gets rejected. A moving excerpt of that moment ends with everyone gathered together with them singing, "We Shall Overcome."

Love also attended the National Women's Conference in Houston in 1977 as a delegate, appointed by Midge Costanza, Jean O'Leary's partner. Costanza was an assistant to President Carter. As Love remembers Costanza, "She deserves a lot of credit for pursuing gay rights, and even the ERA, which Carter indifferently supported while the male colleagues gave her grief. Midge recounts one episode when she invited gay activists to the White House and was asked, 'Does the President know about this?' She replied, 'No, I keep them in the bathroom until he leaves'" (p 152). The Second National Congress to Unite Women is beautifully detailed. The immediacy of tone is what gives the book its propulsive effect; one feels right there at the time with Love in the trenches. "Motions were discussed on abortion, poverty, African-American women, the ERA and other resolutions. The African-American plank was very important…. The ERA was another high-profile issue, hotly contested by Phyllis Schlafly and her group, but all of these resolutions passed. But the emotional focal point was clearly our lesbian rights resolution" (p 153).

Showing how close the lesbian rights quest came to being expunged from the political platform gives us insight into how quickly it can be eradicated. Along with the ERA, and abortion rights, LGBTQ+ rights suffered severe blows during the Trump presidency as he sought to eradicate and undermine LGBTQ+ rights. It is this hindsight in 2021, looking back on 2020, that makes the following words by Love so sobering. She writes, "The lesbian rights plank was modest by today's thinking, calling for an end of discrimination on the basis of sexual and affectional preference in employment, housing, and public accommodations in all states" (p 153).

Written in journalistic style, historic events are interspersed with defining stories of Love's life like magazine features on each subject. For the reader who likes to skip around, this is an ideal format. Love's accomplishments in gay and lesbian activism are many, including establishing and saving Identity House, where LGBTQ+ counseling and support services exist today in New York City. The book shines in its detail, factual rendering, and fearless good humor. It belongs on any reading list of gay and lesbian history.

The Audacity of a Kiss: Love, Art, and Liberation
by **Leslie Cohen**
Rutgers University Press, 2021
Hardcover, 265 pages, $24.95

Reviewed by Roberta Arnold

I could not put down *The Audacity of a Kiss*. Propulsive is often an adjective used to describe a thriller. Leslie Cohen *is* propulsive, and one is easily drawn to her magnetic force. She captures her life in New York city, from her job at Artforum to The Sahara club scene, with striking bravado. I followed her ambitions, her fleeting joys, and her love missives wherever the story went. Though in the end, I had concerns about this book and this mode of narration of our shared lesbian history.

On one hand, *The Audacity of a Kiss* is a story about having the courage to come out, like many of us did, in the early 70s. Certainly, the statue by George Segal in the Christopher Street/Sheridan Square Park, immortalizing Cohen and her partner Beth Siskin, suggests the power of visibility. The fact that the sculpture took thirteen years of hard-fought battles with the city to be allowed to stand is a taste of how long and hard the fight for gay rights takes.

Despite examples of liberation, there are jarring examples of battles we are still fighting, particularly equal justice without regard to race, class, or gender. Cohen's narrative seems oblivious to the realities of contemporary lesbian thinking about race and class. In one instance, Cohen describes a part of Harlem in 1971 as a cartoonish hell when she and her white girlfriend went there in search of a lesbian bar: "menacing Black and brown faces surrounded us, staring.... We stood out like a pair of headlights passing through a dark tunnel" (71). Cohen and her lover found themselves inextricably stranded in a part of Harlem that she depicts as a Hieronymus Bosch painting with no examination of race or ostensible awareness of race and racial justice.

Similarly, Cohen describes a variety of sexist scenes without critique. At a college frat party, one of their friend's tries in vain to wash her foot in the bathroom sink after the foot turned blue from a blue suede shoe. A man took out his penis and arced pee onto her foot. Cohen claims they tried to console their friend, but the absurdity of it all kept them bursting out with "belly laughter" (38).

If sexist encounters were expected at frat parties, they also made regular appearances in the New York business world. When two stereotypical Italian men (dubbed Tweedledee and Tweedledum) claim to be interested in putting up the financial backing for the nightclub, The Sahara, the response from the women (referred to as girls by Cohen) highlights the unexamined sexism. None of the women trying to open the club has any money to put up. The two men demand to know what the women will put up for the club if not money. The women create a mantra, begun as off-the-cuff jargon. One of the women, more savvy to the world of nightclub corruption, perhaps intimately familiar with sex work—as well as stereotypically "sexily" dressed—is singled out in jest: she would give the guys head in exchange for the financial backing.(116) The eruption of class prejudice is glossed over under the guise of a privileged middle class upbringing that allows for the acceptance of a sex worker, --however in bonding together with the others, a tacit separateness shows a dividing line between the two, as though the two groups were on separate teams, the sex worker relegated to a team of her own, a team of one.

As the star power of Cohen grows, so does her defiance of feminist principles. At a fundraising event at The Sahara, when

Patti Smith says "tits," the feminist audience boos and hisses; Cohen singles out this moment as an explanation of the trope of *old guard vs new guard* (176). Cohen continues suggesting that certain disparaging remarks of feminists, calling the club elitist and the women themselves, "fashionable," i.e., "frivolous," denies women a right to "freedom of choice." Is it a choice to perpetuate sexist language that relegates women to body parts? For Cohen, The Sahara Club is at the forefront for the advancement of "broader lesbian culture" (177). She supports this claim citing an address in 1970 by Anselma Dell'Olio, quoted in a 2013 *New Yorker* article by Susan Faludi. "Women's {radical feminist} rage, masquerading as a pseudo-egalitarian radicalism under the 'pro-woman' banner," was turning into "frighteningly vicious anti-intellectual racism of the left" (231-232). While Cohen herself invariably illustrated this argument by degrees throughout the book, the "radical feminist," in brackets, has cursory mention, delegating them as women with "angry rhetoric." The "pseudo-egalitarian radicalism" is demonstrated when the benefit for *Heresies* is given and Cohen inserts a brochure statement in the mailings on why she has famous artwork on the walls of the club, ostensibly as a new feminist venue for artwork: Away from the staid corporate world of museums, art could be looked at through shifting paradigms: from couches, from tables, in rooms filled with dancing women from all class and race backgrounds. "Instead of using angry rhetoric, we were just prowoman, constantly showing what women were capable of, by showcasing their art, music, politics." (178) Indeed, the club was a haven for women-loving women, the beginning of a lesbian place in the city where the mafia did not guard the door. I have a dear Latinx friend who called The Sahara "My second home." She elaborates, "I went there every night they were open, parking myself on the little landing under a light between the first and second floor, watching the parade of women walk by. But they were not my kind of women--they wore lots of make-up, starched shirts, and had done-up hair. I had my paperback in my hand, reading my book and watching, knowing that I was there as an observer. I didn't want to miss anything."

Cohen's embrace of "gritty realism," weaves through the memoir unflinchingly. A term she latches onto after watching Scorsese's 1976 film, "Taxi Driver." Robert De Niro plays a psychopath whose point of view—as seen by the camera from inside his head, dominating the visual effects. Walking out of the movie, Cohen is jazzed, and for several paragraphs uses her eyes as a camera, filming the world around her, including the man on the bus she spots with a tight butt, imagining the fuck (116).

For me as a reader and for the Sinister Wisdom community, lesbianism carries with it a commitment to intersectionality and feminism. *The Audacity of a Kiss* does not share these values. It is through humor and love that Cohen comes closest to intersectionality. At her first meeting with Suskin at Buffalo State, Cohen depicts the villages we live in as seen through the eyes of her mother. What her mother seems to sense intuitively, that the world we live in is made up of different cultural worlds that identify a community fabric, relying on each other to survive, Cohen takes longer to understand. "Suddenly my mother stopped short at an open door, and eyed me with a knowing look. I felt a shift in her demeanor.

Uh-oh.

She had picked up familiar accents drifting out of the room: New York Jews, kindred spirits, descendants of the Shtetls" (25).

Her mother homes in on a voice, the voice of the mother of the woman who is to be Cohen's life partner, and, in effect, this relationship *is* her survival.

There is another heart-warming depiction of Cohen's mother at the unveiling of the Segal statue. Cohen realizes the aide to Mayor Dinkins was someone she had picked up on the subway, and the photographers, journalists, and media frenzy surrounded Cohen & Suskin. "My mother who loved the limelight (it must be hereditary) bobbed her head back and forth between Beth and me, exclaiming: "I am the *Mother!* I am the *Mother!*" (214).

This sweet moment of maternal pride is a counterpoint to some of Cohen's outrageous behavior. When Cohen describes her physical rage: throwing glasses against the wall, yelling, and spewing unhinged anger in the room with an assumed effect of fear in those around her, I no longer believe that her work at The Sahara promotes lesbian equality. The club scene of The Sahara is raw, gritty, and cocaine-laden. The owners installed their drug-dealer in the apartment adjacent to the club, and nick-named the bathroom there as "the boom-boom room," because of the throbbing disco beat reverberating in the toilet seat. The giant coke pile in the apartment was there for any of them to use. In many ways, *The Audacity of a Kiss* is less a story about lesbian equality and more a story of 1980s bar and drug culture.

The interspersing of factual historical events before many of the chapters, along with the footnotes, acknowledges the broader political history and notable feminists who graced the sands of The Sahara at fundraising benefits. Cohen combines the urban cosmopolitan with larger inclusive picture of all classes, races, and sizes combined inside the lesbian entourage of customers who frequented The Sahara. She is a promoter. She promoted her behavior as part of who she was without excuses. Since then, lesbian events have sought a way forward through identification with our Alliances, both with the business venture model like The Dinah to Russian River Women's Weekend to celebrations of Gay Pride. What do our Alliances mean to each one of us? With the rise of intersectionality and a need for allies in this Post-Covid environment, I trust in the knowledge of our foremothers, despite knowing the reasoned mind can make mistakes, I trust in an attempt to come together as a different kind of family—a non-nucleus of differences and trajectories where we can learn from and learn to love one another in the enduring composite of lesbian feminist culture. We have had many rocky starts and falls, and some far-reaching accomplishments, but all in all, the work continues, and one might say: The Audacity of Sisterhood itself continues, with its plucky embrace of Alliances. Leslie Cohen's memoir shines a light of recognition on some of the dark corners and brave beginnings of this Sisterhood.

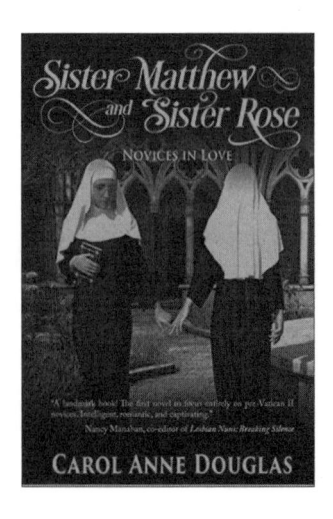

Sister Matthew and Sister Rose, Novices in Love by **Carol Anne Douglas**
Hermione Books, 2021,
308 pages, paperback, $14.99

Reviewed by Suzanne Barbara

I began this book expecting fiction but finding a history of my experience as a girl growing up in pre-Vatican II Catholicism. At first, it was very difficult to go there. It was a small world, especially for women, whose ideas, hopes, and feelings were suppressed in all the ways Sister Matthew and Sister Rose encountered. In fact, since both women had been to secular colleges before entering, suppression was necessary; for women who went straight from twelve years of Catholic school to the convent, if they were "good girls," their identity was already formed in line with the convent values we see in Douglas' book. No individuality to suppress!

Many times, the method and degree of suppression reminded me of Philip Pullman's "The Golden Compass," wherein characters within an unnamed religious group kidnapped children and conducted experiments that separated them from their animal "familiar." This alienation from a vital part of the child (probably their very soul) turned him or her into a zombie-like being who never recovered and eventually died. The repressive Catholicism of the '50s and '60s had the same effect on the soul.

The fact that the main characters had a four-year college experience before entering explains their ability to think critically about their convent experience. Sister Matthew entered as a "seeker," exploring the question of God's existence. Sister Rose's motivation was emotional, being romantically attached to the ritual, the beautiful convent setting and the value of an all-woman community. As Reverend Mother pointed out, "You are in love with the convent."

The brilliant plot device of time travel makes possible an exploration of the main characters' relationship in a setting that, as described, would never allow this (although I've heard many stories over the years of successful convent romances.) Because their relationship was strengthened and nourished in this "time out of time," the plot resolution is believable. I did, however, wish for more time for character development toward the end of the novel, to solidify and make visible their progression toward radical change.

Overall, I applaud Douglas for her historic realism in this pre-modern period of the Catholic world, and her sensitivity to the main characters' emotional experiences. As their church made the transition from medieval to modern, her characters transitioned from lives of unconscious patriarchy to being fully themselves. It would be pleasant to see how their future selves played out.

Where There Are Mountains
by **Sarah F. Pearlman**
Paperback $15

Reviewed by Roberta Arnold

A young lesbian architect unearths the bones of two females in an embrace. Among the many bones found in Greece, this was a rare exciting find, and one that might not stay as such: two sets of bones locked together, at the hands of patriarchal Greek decision-makers. The young archeologist is in a quandary about handing over the bones to the Greek Authority, and she decides to says nothing. She secures the site and leaves the cave to go back home.

The story of the architect bookends three narratives of matrilineal tribes travelling on the road South, towards "The sun lands, *Ilios*...." (15). These matrilineal tribes were subjected to attacks by the warring male-dominated patriarchal tribes, tribes who worshipped a male god, but the matrilineal tribes persisted, at times banding together and becoming stronger in size. When the first matrilineal tribe in the first narrative finds relative safety along the route, they dance and celebrate their goddess, *Ge*, a female deity who represents Nature, Dance, and Desire. In this respect, and in the divided struggle to hold onto their worldview, the imagined goddesses in *Where There Are Mountains* by Sarah F. Pearlman parallels the Sumerian Goddess, Inanna, artfully detailed in Judy Grahn's latest book, *Eruptions of Inanna*. Through thorough research, Grahn explores the female deity Inanna, worshipped by peace-loving Sumerian poets from 3100 BCE to 2100 BCE in *Eruptions of Inanna*, A Sapphic Classic from *Sinister Wisdom* and Nightboat Books.

Pearlman's novella imagines both a matrilineal and matriarchal people worshipping female deities during the Neolithic age, seven thousand years ago, on a path near Mount Olympus in Greece. The first narrator, Janija, describes her tribe relishing the splendors of nature before thanking their goddess, *Ge*. "Flower-covered fields perfumed the air with their sweet scent—accompanying us as we walked. Orange-gold sunsets spreading across the sky. Stars decorating the blackness of night" (15). Their tribe, like the worshippers of Inanna, were joyful and desirous. Dancing and sexual pleasures were an accepted expression of their bodies. "Rolling our hips as if we were *erojai*. Lovers. Love-making. Mimicking women rubbing against women..." (15). But, not only women with women. Women with men also. These tribal eruptions could be seen in a similar light to the ancient goddess Innana, although in Pearlman's tales the goddesses are three. First, a fictional one named *Ge* and in the later chapters, we meet the second two goddesses, entwined together as one, the deity of the matriarchal tribe.

The attacks of the warring tribes are hard to take in as Pearlman vividly describes them. Rape and capture of women as slaves is commonplace on the path southward. *Where There Are Mountains* is also a story of resilience and love of a daughter for her mother. Ayala, the second narrator, daughter from her mother's horrific attack and rape, ties herself to her mother by keeping her in her sight. Ayala finds herself being given to one of the less brutal men by her mother, because, since they have both become slaves, this makes it inevitable that Ayala will be taken by one of the men in the tribe that captured them. Through this spare joyless life, Ayala learns to fight, to time her escape, and to feed her mother in her mother's dying sickness and be there for her, kissing her goodbye on the mouth before she sleeps into her death (35).

Ayala escapes to join a tribe that worships two female deities entwined and has to be guided to learn to be unafraid. The 3rd narrative is the story of Ayala and Eyann, two women from different tribes who become lovers. Eyann teaches Ayala to look at herself without hatred for how she had escaped—her escape had led to more killing and had led the warring patriarchal tribe to the matriarchal tribe, a tribe consisting almost entirely of women. Ayala had to see her light skin without hatred and let go of the hardness in her heart. The parallel to colonialist subterfuge comes to mind when reading this part.

Eventually, Eyann succeeded in bringing happiness into Ayala's heart, and for the first time Ayala learns what it feels like to have a mouth between her legs. Eyann's tribe is made up of not just one mother but many mothers, Eyann explains to Ayala, after a big gathering celebrating the two combined female deities of worship. "Ayala, I am from a strong mother-line.... I have many mothers. The mother who birthed me. Her sisters. Their oldest daughters. I drank at many breasts" (63).

Eyann's matriarchal tribe, The *Atai*, are the longest enduring tribe in this novella. We are enlightened about the title of this book in the heading of their chapter on page 41. *Where there are mountains, people are not easily subdued.* In the last chapter, the present day archeologist goes home to her lesbian partner, bemoaning her imagined dreaded fate of the unearthed skeletons of two women intertwined, her partner tells her, she did well: the lesbian skeletons remained in the cave. Bureaucratic foot-dragging came to a fruitful end, it happened, and the skeletons remained in the cave. When the press got hold of the story, the tourist attraction would bring in much-needed money to an austere Greece. The two women celebrated in a toast to another *Lesvos*, the Sapphic Island. As the Epilogue quotation from Sappho proclaims on page 81, "*Someone will remember us, even in another time.*" And, to be sure, in this imagined gem of a novella, they did.

REMEMBRANCES

Ellen Louise Spangler

By Emily Greene

Ellen Louise Spangler was born January 22, 1934 in Bloomington, Illinois and passed on peacefully, Aug 8, 2021 at the home she and Mary Alice Stout, her partner of thirty-two years, had built in Alapine, a twenty-four-year-old Lesbian community in Alabama. She was surrounded by Mary Alice, her daughter Carla, and their little dog Bitsy.

Ellen Spangler and Mary Alice Stout

Beginning in the 1960s and throughout her life Ellen fought for equality and justice for all people, especially for women. She was one of the founders of Hubbard House in 1976, the first domestic violence shelter in Jacksonville, Florida. She was the mother of four children and always found time to spend with them, their spouses, five grandchildren and seven great-grandchildren, with joy and comfort.

Ellen Spangle

Ellen was an experienced carpenter. I first met her in 1980 as she was remodeling one of the cottages at the Pagoda, a Lesbian community in St. Augustine, Florida. Ellen built the stage in the Pagoda community center, which led to the wonderful Lesbian cultural center of music, dance and plays. Ellen was an accomplished pianist and in the 1970s built a harpsicord and volunteered at her children's school to play and lead sing-alongs.

In 1984 when she turned fifty, the Pagoda had a big celebration and croning for both Ellen and Rose. In the mid 1980s she lived on a farm with goats, chickens and a veggie garden with Rose in Williston, Florida. In 1987 she moved to Anderson, South Carolina. After studying with Kaymora, Ellen went on to start Starcrest, a spiritual and psychic center. Ellen also helped organize the Upstate Women's Community and served as a substitute teacher in a Clemson Religious Class, as well as teaching many classes at Starcrest. It is here that she met her life-long partner, Mary Alice in 1989 while teaching a class, in Knoxville, Tennessee. Their commitment ceremony was held at Starcrest with more than one hundred friends and family.

Sheeba Mountain Properties, Incorporated, comprised of three Lesbians from the Pagoda, bought 188 acres in Alabama, of which 108 acres were surveyed but undeveloped two-acre plots that became Alapine. In 1997 Mary Alice and Ellen were the first to move to Alapine. At this point they were both focused on climate change and how they could lessen their carbon footprint, which led them to build, with only minimal help from a male friend, their earth sheltered home, with berm roof, rainwater collection for their water supply and composting toilets.

Both Mary Alice and Ellen gave much time and energy to helping create Alapine Lesbian community, being part of organizing, attending meetings, setting up game nights and donated land for the Alapine community center. They were part of the founding mothers of Mountain Mamas, an all-women's craft store, started in 1996 which grew to have eighty women's arts and crafts on Lookout Mountain. They attended Land Dyke Gatherings in Virginia and Missouri, as well as the OLOC gatherings in North Carolina and Tampa, Florida. Ellen and Emily were invited to speak to the Queer History Class at the University of Alabama, Tuscaloosa, which resulted in nine students coming to Alapine for a weekend to help with Alapine projects in 2010. Ellen and Mary Alice will both be remembered for their graciousness in sharing their home for community meals, parties, and dances. Along with Mary Alice, there will be many friends and her loving family who will miss her dearly.

Remembrance: Marcia Freedman
May 17, 1938-September 21, 2021

By Irena Klepfisz

I met Marcia for the first time in 1989 when she spoke to the Jewish Committee to End the Occupation (JWCEO), a New York City-based support group for the Israeli Women in Black who were protesting Israeli government's response to the first Intifada and its policies in the West Bank and Gaza. Marcia was invited to speak. In my introduction, I admitted: "I don't know when you came out, Marcia, I just know you started doing *it* before I did." I looked anxiously at Marcia and saw her grinning that incredible Marcia smile that always emerged at a moment's notice. At the time, JWCEO was struggling to publicize Women in Black's existence and perspective. Marcia believed in our mission and quickly arranged for a grant that enabled us to print and distribute a newsletter publicizing women and peace activities throughout the U.S. and Israel/Palestine, to strengthen ties between individual Jewish and Palestinian feminist and lesbian activists, to arrange tours for Israeli and Palestinian women speakers here and to send JWCEO representatives on extended visits overseas. In short, Marcia, without an official position, became largely responsible for spreading the news of anti-government protests in Israel and parallel protests here by Jewish women.

At the time of this first meeting, I knew Marcia was a major figure. I recognized that: she was a Jew and a dyke; she was an outspoken feminist; she had moved to Israel in 1967 and served in the Kensset (Israeli Parliament); and she was a Jew who publicly insisted that Palestinian citizens' rights be recognized and respected. Here's some of what I didn't know about the work Marcia had done between her arrival and departure from Israel in 1981:

- she served in the Knesset from 1974-1977 as—till then—the first American born Knesset member and as one of three representatives of the Citizens Rights Movement (Ratz) led by Shulamit Aloni;
- she co-founded the Women's Party in Israel;
- she worked to liberalize abortion laws and the eventual legalization of abortion;
- she helped found the first shelter for battered (Haifa);

- she opened the first women's bookstore in Israel (Haifa);
- she introduced discussions and bills and allotted money to address for the first time in Israel domestic abuse, rape and incest (Knesset members often laughed, saying none of these were problems in Jewish homes);
- she addressed the issue of teen prostitution and enlarged the Youth Ministry Budget to support young girls;
- she expressed her solidarity with Palestinian citizens of Israel and those living in the Occupied Territories;
- she co-founded and helped run the Kol Ha-Isha Women's Center (Haifa).

It's an astonishing record for a woman who was working in a country that prided itself on and publicized its alleged gender equality and which consistently refused to acknowledge that women in Israel faced the same abuses and inequities that women in other countries were addressing. Looking at both what she identified as issues and what she actually accomplished, it's obvious why Marcia is remembered and honored in Israel as one of the founders of its feminist movement.

But Marcia didn't retire after returning to the U.S. and settling in the Bay Area. Over the next thirty-five years, she:

- created the Women's Computer Literacy Project;
- became the director of marketing for the American Society on Aging (ASC);
- through ASC, established the Lesbian and Gay Aging Issues Network;
- co-founded Bay Area Women in Black;
- co-founded Brit Tzedek v'Shalom and served as its president, advocating for the establishment of a Palestinian state and for Jerusalem as a shared capital;
- became a member of Ashby Village and its Board of Directors, a nonprofit that serves seniors and helps them stay independent in their homes;

- founded Elder Action whose members focused on social justice issues;
- became a member of the Board and President of the San Francisco Film Festival.

Between 1997 and 2002, Marcia made yearly trips to Israel for extended stays. She co-founded and oversaw the Community School for Women (Jerusalem) which taught women's studies courses and practical skills to poor and underserved minority women.

My working experience with Marcia began in 2002 when she drew me into the newly formed New York chapter of Brit Tzedek. I have vivid memories of long, difficult meetings and during breaks Marcia and I would take walks and talk—not only about the issues raised in the meeting, but everything else. Marcia had this incredible knack of being able to move almost seamlessly from politics to the personal, the artistic, to gossip. She knew how to unwind, step back and refresh.

In a thread on Facebook started by Aliza Becker, Director of the American Jewish Peace Archive, many friends and fellow activists paid tribute to Marcia, frequently noting her height at 4' 8". Here is a sample of some of their comments.

We loved her for her courage and determination, the 'small, still voice that makes itself heard.'

I remember many a time when Marcia was with me for contentious meetings with community critics. We were fighting the good fight for justice and to have a voice at the table. She was my ally in fundraising, strategizing, gossiping and bolstering each other.

One of Marcia's many super powers was that while presenting as mild and unthreatening, she was often the most dangerous mind in the room (dangerous, that is, to systems of injustice).

I learned so much from her about how to approach conflict, not just political but within the movement itself: stay focused, don't get distracted by other's *mishegas*, and reserve your energy for the fights that mattered.

Marcia and I were occasionally at opposite ends of the political spectrum, and so our meetings were sometimes heated — but I respected her feistiness, her deep commitment, her pragmatism, her experience, her dogged determination to make a difference.

Marcia didn't wear her accomplishments on her sleeve. She didn't seek outsize attention for herself. She wrote and spoke simply and without pomp. Her thoughts were always detailed, balanced, and delivered calmly even during times of violence.

I remember being immediately impressed by the soft-spoken dynamism of this diminutive woman who emerged from a pack of passionate, opinionated Jews as the obvious choice to lead this nascent organization [Brit Tzedek].

Nothing reflects Marcia's loyalty to her friends more than her devotion to Esther Broner and her family. I'm not sure when they met, but they experienced the Israel of the 1970s together and shared in that period's emerging feminism. In 1985, Esther published *A Weave of Women*, a novel that evokes the excitement, chaos and struggles of passionate feminists trying to transform Israeli society. Marcia produced her own impressions of the the same period in her memoir *Exile in the Promised Land* in 1990. In her acknowledgement, the first person she mentions is Esther's support of her writing. When Esther and her husband began having health crises, Marcia flew repeatedly from California to help. And she stayed with Esther during her last illness and was with her when she died.

I have taught both the novel and the memoir. They're interesting to read side by side, the first rooted in magic realism, the second rooted in political history. Marcia's memoir provides the historical background for Esther's novel and many students found it useful in understanding the novel's complex plot structure.

But *Exile* is not simply a historical record. It is also a very sharp-elbowed account of the personal and political difficulties of an activist. One thing that is evident in *Exile* is what Marcia is not: she's never romantic about politics—mainstream or movement. And she's never romantic about her own personal conflicts. Throughout Marcia is open about the complications and complexities of organizing, of working collectively, of creating alliances, of trying to create change while maintaining balanced family relations and friendships.

In *Exile*, Marcia also includes descriptions of her daughter Jenny's pain in dealing with the Israeli public's ridicule and contempt for her mother. When Marcia comes out, Jenny declares it's the last straw and insists on going to live with her father in California. Later, when Marcia returns to the U.S., she and Jenny reconcile, and Jenny finds her mother is a heroine to American feminists.

My students were mainly eighteen- to twenty-year-old women who admired Marcia as an activist, but were upset by its effect on Jenny. These were young women who believed in activism and also expected to be mothers. They struggled with the idea of the "mother activist/activist mother»—what she owed her family and children, what she owed society, and in what way these were intertwined. Our discussions of the "mother citizen's" responsibility to society were some of the most important discussions I had with these students. Let's remember what many of Marcia's obituaries omit. Marcia was not only a mother activist who drew scorn because of her political and feminist positions; she was also an out lesbian, something unheard of in Israel (and almost everywhere else) in the 1970s. In *Exile*, Marcia never sugar-coats either her own or Jenny's feelings or actions. Lesbian mothers of Marcia's generation, no matter where they lived, inevitably exposed their daughters to the cruelty of others. And yet, it is because of activist and lesbian mothers like Marcia and the strengths of daughters like Jenny that we now have open lesbian and gay families. We are all indebted to Marcia *and* Jenny for getting us to where we are today.

Marcia Freedman: *May her memory be a blessing.*

CONTRIBUTORS

Sus Austill is a licensed clinical social worker healing people from trauma through narrative therapy. Her own life is a rich blend of being honored listener to stories and living the stories that others tell. She draws strength from her love of women, writing, and art.

Woody Blue was transplanted to Gainesville, FL, in 1992 and grew roots. She is a radical peace activist and lesbian-feminist. Womonwrites inspired her to blossom as a writer and an artist. Lesbian community is her strength. Documenting lesbian herstory is sacred. Love and hope sustain her in her female-centric world.

Helen Renée Brawner is an Arkansas native raised in Memphis, who has written since childhood. Western North Carolina became home in 1972. Love of nature and words bind her to southern Appalachia's diversity and to traditions of sharing lesbian community and writing birthed at Womonwrites, the Southeast Lesbian Writers' Conference, 1979–2019.

B. Leaf Cronewrite is the crone name of Maryann Hopper. She knows that name-claiming and all kinds of lesbians' stories are valuable. She came out in 1977 in Memphis surrounded by supportive lesbians. Now in Atlanta, she hangs out with creative souls who inspire her to write stories set in the South.

Kathleen "Corky" Culver loves attending circles, especially under the stars. A pollinator of lesbian feminist ideals, she has introduced women to music, dance, sobriety, and each other! Her book of poetry, *The Natural Law of Water*, is available online, and *Finding the Well* will be released soon.

Dancingwater is a visual artist, cremation urn designer, writer, and dyke who lives in a cohousing community in Atlanta, Georgia.

Gwen Demeter has spent most of her life living collectively in womyn's community. She and Gail Atkins, her partner of forty years, moved to Mississippi thirty-eight years ago and bought land with the intention of creating womyn's community. They built their house, their road, and their life with many other women at Silver Circle.

Kim Duckett was born in Appalachia and at eighteen cofounded the first rape crisis center in Asheville, NC. She now holds a PhD in women's studies and transpersonal psychologies. Author of *The Wheel of the Year as an Earth-Based Spiritual Psychology for Women*, an ordained priestess in Dianic goddess and Wiccan traditions, she may be found at kimduckett.com.

Barbara Esrig moved to Gainesville, came out, and started working at the Gainesville Women's Health Center in October 1979. She's been politically active in the womyn's community since then. She worked twenty years as writer-in-residence in an arts-in-medicine program, listening to patient's stories and writing their oral histories. She is happily retired, writing and cooking.

Laurel Ferejohn now makes more time for her own writing. She has had some success with fiction, memoirs in literary journals, and won a prize or two, which have brought needed encouragement to finish her novel. Her work appears in *Quiddity International*, *Southeast Review*, and *Thomas Wolfe Review*.

Drea Firewalker, as a crone, realizes that standing in her power gives her the right to be bold, claim her wisdom, and pursue her life as she wishes. She creates glass art, tends her flower gardens, holds powerful rituals for womyn, travels the world, and loves this life.

Lorraine Fontana is a working-class dyke from Queens, NY, a supporter of Black empowerment, and an antiwar activist. A VISTA worker in 1968, she came to Atlanta with other left-feminist women to found the Atlanta Lesbian Feminist Alliance (ALFA). She used her legal training at the People's College of Law at GA Legal Services, the EEOC, and Lambda Legal.

Phyllis Free is an artist, activist, and percussionist who specializes in creative collaborations with other arts professionals. She incorporates poetry, visual arts, music, and theatre into community exhibitions, arts residencies, and performances and partnerships that address social justice and feminist themes. Contact her at Phyllis Free/Creative Services at phylfree@mindspring.com.

Debra L. Gish is an international development practitioner engaged in multiple disciplines: women's, elders', and indigenous rights, gender-based violence, transformative justice. A published memoir, *Displaced*; poetry in *Best American Poets*; author/editor of *Crone Chronicles 20-20: Intimately Inspiring Glimpses into the Lives of Wise Women 52+*, a collection of stories by female elders.

Cedar Heartwood was born in 1949 in northern Louisiana, came out in 1973, and has lived on wimmin's land most of the time since 1988. Her degree was in sociology, and her career has been varied, with writing her anchor. Now retired, she has time to push for progressive-leaning change in her rural county.

Mendy Knott lives in Burnsville, NC. She is an award-winning screenplay writer and poet. Her works include: *A Little Lazarus* (Half Acre Press, 2010); *Across the ARK-LA-TEX: A Cross Family Cookbook* (Limbertwig Press, 2010); editor of *Raising Voices: A Café of Our Own Anthology* (Burning Bush Press, 1997).

Lenny Lasater grew up in northwest Tennessee and now lives with her all-time love partner, Sid Robinson, in Atlanta, GA. She was a coal miner for a year and is now a master electrician at Lenny Lasater Electrical. She is also a singer/songwriter/bassist with Just Roxie (www.justroxienow.com).

Judy L. McVey was born in Columbia, SC, and raised in Chattanooga, TN, and Atlanta, GA. She is a retired orchestra teacher and pastoral counselor and lived out her dream with her partner of thirty-one years on their land in east Georgia, Pteradyktil.

Marilyn Mesh is a Jewish lesbian, hippie organic watermelon farmer, teacher in a women's prison, director of a rural health clinic. Blessed to love work, blessed to be retired and having fun. Hot weather, mosquitoes = no joy. Joy = wife, community, grandkids, and alternative ways to honor her Judaism.

Sage Morse lives in St. Petersburg, FL, and teaches for the Hospital/Homebound Program of Pinellas County Schools. She is active with the teachers' union and takes pleasure in hassling state legislators as a union representative. She was contributor to and co-editor of *Womyn's Words*, a St. Petersburg, FL, feminist newsletter, from 1982 until its final edition in 2010.

Merril Mushroom grew up in Miami Beach in the 1940s and came out there in the 1950s. She lived in New York City in the 1960s and has lived in rural Tennessee since the 1970s. She has written a variety of prose pieces. Her old-timey bar dyke stories can be found in out-of-print lesbian publications from the 1980s and 1990s.

Rose Norman is a retired professor of English and women's studies who has co-edited all six SLFAHP special issues. As general editor of the SLFAHP, she interviewed over one hundred lesbians, and is writing a book about the Pagoda, a lesbian intentional community and cultural center in St. Augustine, FL. She is a native Alabamian.

Cat Purdom is an art director in Nashville, TN, who specializes in package design. She is a dreamer who loves spending time in nature, journaling, exploring her spirituality, meditating, and writing poems and music.

Gail Reeder grew up everywhere. She returned South following familial feet to rural North Carolina. Her writings on social injustices appeared in the *Quicksilver Times*, *Southern Voice*, and other publications. "These days I am more dangerous with a pickax than a gun, but I still keep an eye on the revolution."

Diana Rivers, born in 1933, lives on women's land in Arkansas. She authored the seven-novel *Hadra Series*, is a Lambda Literary Award finalist, and winner of the Golden Crown Literary Award for Speculative Fiction. She is an ecofeminist, active in peace and justice movements, and originated events to empower women in arts.

Flash Silvermoon was a wild, irreverent Piscean witch and has transitioned to untamed dimensions. She drums with her beloved animals and spirit guides regularly, concocting magic and music and sprinkling it on her earthly lovers and friends. When you see crystals, water, and fire, think of her. She will be there.

Maya White Sparks has served as writer/editor for a feminist psychologist since 1980. She wrote and coproduced the CD *Meditations with Maya, Sound Dimension* by Cheryl Jacobs. For twenty-five years, she edited Spiral Grove's newsletter, *Close to Mother Earth*. She currently serves on the Grove's Board and is transforming with the advent of the Aquarian Age (mayawhitesparks.net).

Robin Toler has a feminist therapy practice in Louisiana based on the principles of equity and human rights. She offers addictions counseling, trauma resolution, and art therapy. She plays shekere in Bloco Jacaré, a samba group. She enjoys making art, writing, traveling, and teaching. Contact her at www.robintoler.com and www.robintolerartstudio.com.

Jenny Yates is a freelance astrologer currently living in Rockville, MD, with her Venezuelan wife. She writes all the time, whether it's astrological interpretations, personal pieces, or poetry. For the last few years, she has been working on a novel.

Beth York is a retired music professor from Converse College, Spartanburg, SC. Ladyslipper Music produced her *Transformations*; she performed the ensemble piece at national and international women's music festivals. Her latest recording, *Finding Home* (2019), contains original songs by Beth, Barbara Ester, and Phyllis Free. Available through Amazon, eyork4366@gmail.com, and CDBaby.com.

BOLD Ideas, ESSENTIAL Reading

"I remember Sahara as a spring in the desert of the time!"
—Gloria Steinem

"Leslie's tribute to Sahara is testimony to the sanctuary we found in being together, feeling safe and enthralled by a sense of freedom. Whether you found that in The Duchess, Bonnie and Clyde's or The Cubbyhole, this is your invitation to revisit. Little compared with the sense of anticipation you felt walking through the door and into the glances, stares or smiles of women and that the next few hours held countless possibilities."
—Ginny Apuzzo, gay rights and AIDS activist and former executive director of the National LGBTQ Task Force

"Beautifully written.... I love Leslie's book. The detail she gives is remarkable both about her relationship with Beth, the beginning of Sahara where I spent many an amazing evening, and even her days in Siena. Leslie brings it all back to life. Reading this book, I was brought back to the Upper East Side in the '70s. Leslie had a magnetic power, and it suffuses the pages of this book."
—Brenda Feigen, feminist activist, film producer, attorney, cofounder of Ms. Magazine

"Bold, beautiful and brutally honest. [Cohen] writes as she has lived, without fear or hesitation."
—Brooke Kennedy, Emmy Award nominated television producer and director

"Sahara was the only female place that I felt comfortable as I identified with the atmosphere and the women who patronized it—fashionable, glamorous, and happy."
—Patricia Field, Emmy Award-winning costume designer, stylist and fashion designer

THE AUDACITY OF A KISS
Love, Art, and Liberation
Leslie Cohen
$24.94 cloth

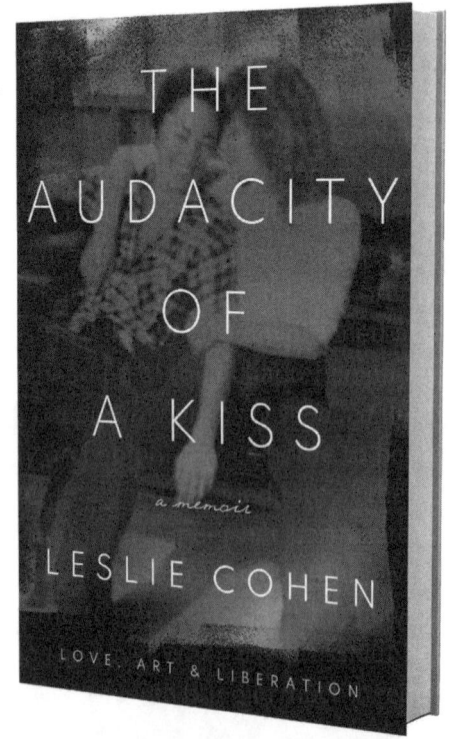

RUTGERS UNIVERSITY PRESS
30% off and free shipping. Use code RLCOHEN.
Discount valid sitewide.
www.rutgersuniversitypress.org

Sinister Wisdom
A Multicultural Lesbian Literary & Art Journal

SUBSCRIBE TODAY!

Subscribe using the enclosed subscription card or online at
www.SinisterWisdom.org/subscribe using PayPal

Or send check or money order to
Sinister Wisdom - 2333 McIntosh Road, Dover, FL 33527-5980

Sinister Wisdom accepts gifts of all sizes to support the journal.

Sinister Wisdom is free on request to women in prisons and psychiatric institutions.

Back issues available!

Sinister Wisdom **Back Issues Available**

123	A Tribute to Conditions ($14)
122	Writing Communities ($14)
121	Eruptions of Inanna ($17.95)
120	Asian Lesbians ($14)
118	Forty-five Years: A Tribute to the Lesbian Herstory Archives ($14)
114	A Generous Spirit ($18.95)
108	For The Hard Ones. Para las duras ($18.95)
107	Black Lesbians— We Are the Revolution! ($14)
104	Lesbianima Rising: Lesbian-Feminist Arts in the South, 1974–96 ($12)
103	Celebrating the Michigan Womyn's Music Festival ($12)
102	The Complete Works of Pat Parker ($22.95) Special Limited edition hardcover ($35)
98	Landykes of the South ($12)
96	What Can I Ask ($18.95)
93	Southern Lesbian-Feminist Herstory 1968–94 ($12)
91	Living as a Lesbian ($17.95)
88	Crime Against Nature ($17.95)
80	Willing Up and Keeling Over
54	Lesbians & Religion
50	Not the Ethics Issue
49	The Lesbian Body
48	Lesbian Resistance Including work by Dykes in Prison
47	Lesbians of Color: Tellin' It Like It 'Tis

46	Dyke Lives
45	Lesbians & Class (the first issue of a lesbian journal edited entirely by poverty and working class dykes)
43/44	15th Anniversary double-size (368 pgs) retrospective
-	Sister Love: The Letters of Audre Lorde and Pat Parker ($14.95)
-	Notes for a Revolutión ($14)

Back issues are $6.00 unless noted plus $3.00 Shipping & Handling for 1st issue; $1.00 for each additional issue.
Order online at www.sinisterwisdom.org

Or mail check or money order to:
Sinister Wisdom
2333 McIntosh Road
Dover, FL 33527-5980